more RAILROADS you can model

EDITED BY MIKE SCHAFER

Track planning for railroads
you'd like to model — page 2
Monon — page 4
Graham County Railroad — page 16
B&M's Gloucester branch — page 23
McCloud River Railroad — page 28
PRR's Horseshoe Curve — page 34
Milwaukee Road's Beer Line — page 46
White Pass & Yukon — page 53
Maryland & Pennsylvania — page 60
Chicago Aurora & Elgin — page 68
Bibliography — page 76

FRONT COVER SCENES: (Top photo) Glistening from an encounter with a brief June thunderstorm, Monon's Chicago-to-Louisville *Thoroughbred* greets sunlight again at Gosport, Ind. Nearby, a Pennsylvania Railroad freight ambles southward. The 1953 scene was built in 1978 by Mike Schafer, with assistance by Gary Dolzall, Bob Hayden, and Mont Switzer. Photo by A. L. Schmidt. (Bottom photo) Chicago Aurora & Elgin interurban cars pose at the R.E.L.I.C. trolley museum near South Elgin, Ill., for nighttime photographers of the North Western Illinois Chapter — National Railway Historical Society in 1969. Photo by Mike Schafer.

ART DIRECTOR: Lawrence Luser
CONTINUITY: Donnette Dolzall, Mike Schafer
LAYOUT: Bill Scholz

KALMBACH BOOKS

First printing, 1978. Second printing, 1979.

© 1978 by Kalmbach Publishing Co. This book may not be reproduced in part or in whole without written permission from the publisher, except in the case of brief quotations used in reviews. Published by Kalmbach Publishing Co., 1027 North Seventh Street, Milwaukee, WI 53233. Printed in U.S.A. Library of Congress Catalog Card Number: 77-86274. ISBN: 0-89024-534-7.

MODEL RAILROADER: A. L. Schmidt.

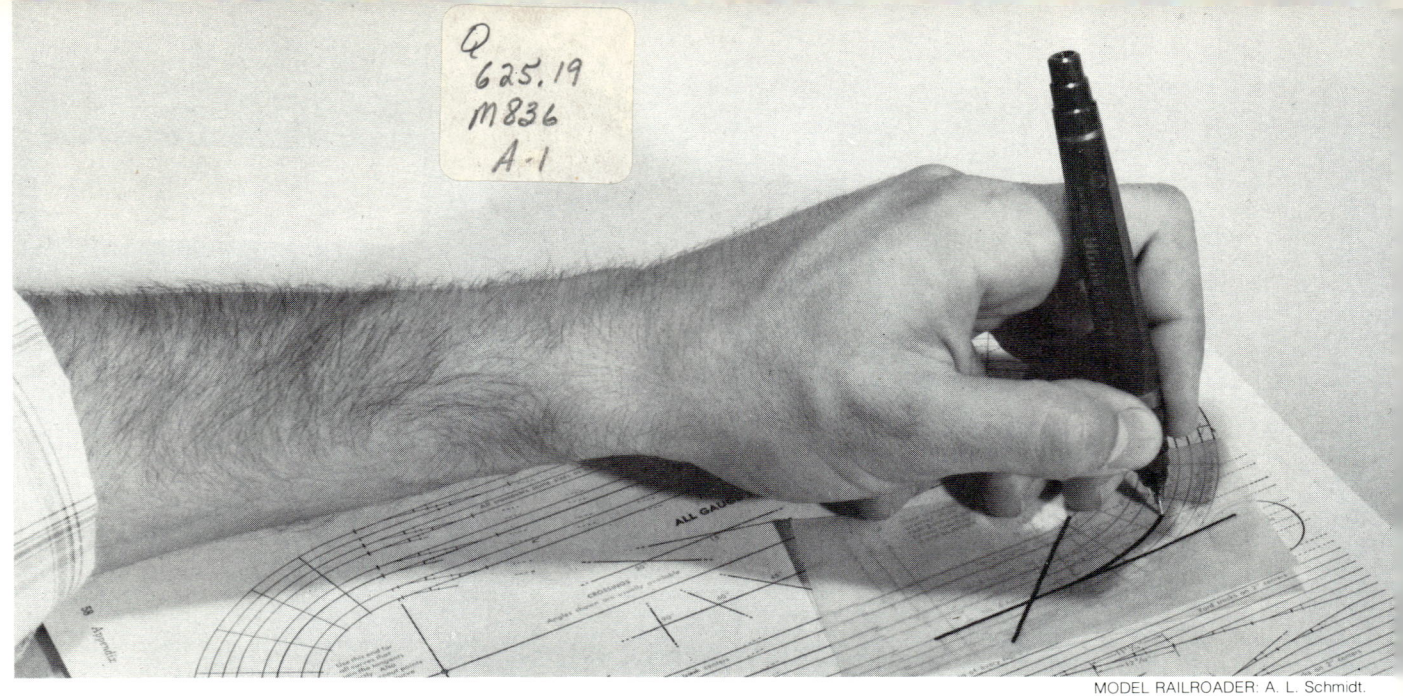

Track planning for railroads you'd like to model

Modeling the prototype exactly isn't easy—it's impossible

EVERY chapter in this book includes a suggested track plan for the featured prototype railroad, but many readers may want to develop their own track plan or at least alter ours to meet their own requirements and desires. Once you get the knack of it, track planning becomes still another enjoyable aspect of model railroading. Let us offer some helpful hints.

A critique of track plans

We have studied many of the track plans that have been published over the years (including many in our own books and magazines). We concluded that the following are some of the most common problems found in many track designs:

• Too much is crammed into the space available.

• Not enough places for car switching are provided.

• Too much space is devoted to yards, too little to scenery.

• Some plans have so many switches that the average person could not maintain all of them.

• Too often, tracks parallel the walls or other tracks, making the space appear smaller than it is.

• Usually the edges of the benchwork are made straight, when they would be better curving wider here, narrower there.

• Some plans include trapped aisles, when the same space could be arranged with an E, C, L, F, or other shape that allows you to walk freely to any part of the layout except the center of a turnback curve.

Track planning guidelines

In designing a model railroad layout for a given space in the house or garage, consider the plan and the prototype separately. Then you will have some idea of what your limitations are going to be and you will be in a better position to make intelligent decisions.

The first step in your planning is to determine how much space is available. Allow as much space as you can for the layout. Even if you want a "simple layout," meaning perhaps less than 15 track switches (the number of track switches rather than layout size usually determines the complexity of a layout), it is far better to put the switches and their connecting tracks into a big space rather than a small one. A small layout with 15 switches may not be simple at all to design.

At first it may appear that very little space can be spared for your layout. Before conceding that only a small model railroad can be built, consider devices that pull the layout out of the way when not in use if such trickery will allow you to make the layout larger. Some modelers have designed layouts that can be pulled up to the ceiling when not in use; others have devised ways to fold the layout against a wall between operating sessions. If the layout is to fold up, try to retain one level part so you don't have to take all the rolling stock off the track.

Next, plan the aisles. *Aisles are more important than the track routings.* We usually have more flexibility in positioning the tracks than in locating the aisles. Avoid trapped aisles that must be reached by ducking under the tablework. They may be necessary in the centers of return loops but usually not in other areas.

Consider your aisle borders as negotiable. Draw them with dashed lines, not solid. You can take away some aisle space to make a track fit, adding aisle space elsewhere to compensate.

Look at the prototype

After roughly planning your space and aisles, turn your thoughts to the prototype. Consider making a field trip to the prototype armed with a notebook, pencil, and perhaps a camera, but be sure not to trespass on railroad property. Most of your note-taking and photography can be accomplished from overhead bridges, nearby roads, and public crossings. Make sketches or take pictures of prototype track arrangements, structure locations, and other items that will be pertinent to designing a track plan that will capture the flavor of the railroad. If you can't get out to see the prototype, check books and magazines for information and photographs.

Consider in what ways the prototype is ideal for modeling. Make the most of those features. Here is where *selective compression* comes in. We explained selective compression in RAILROADS YOU CAN MODEL, but for those of you who don't yet have that book, we'll explain this ever-important principle again: Selective compression means incorporating the most interesting or unique qualities of the prototype into a model layout of manageable size.

Other things need to be considered, too. Ask yourself these questions:
• Will the structures along the line be interesting?
• Will the trains have interesting makeup?
• Will the scenery have variety and intrigue?
• Is operation going to be varied, or are pretty much the same movements going to be repeated day after day? (That would soon lead to monotony.)
• Are there prototype track features I would like to reproduce?

Don't try to follow the prototype faithfully. You can't. You can specialize on the part of the prototype that you like most at the expense of other parts, but you must make sacrifices to do it, so be aware of this. If railroad modeling is more important to you, you will tend to make ground plans of stations and other structures more nearly to scale. But if model railroading is more important, you must condense their sizes. Either is correct. Neither is ideal.

Things to avoid

If you want realistic operation and a good overall effect, the following track-plan features should be avoided as much as possible:
• Large yards.
• Double-ended yards (switches to all tracks at both ends).
• Large roundhouses.
• Provisions for running long trains. They make station tracks longer and distances between stations seem ridiculously short.
• Long straight lines.
• Long straight tracks. It's better to use very gradual curves for that same distance.
• Helter-skelter track routing. When one station has to be close to another or to an unrelated yard, try to arrange a scenic feature between the two to separate them visually. Bridges, short tunnels, highway overpasses, or a bit of dense woods will do.
• Too many route options. Plans with many diverse routes may be interesting to look at, but their prototype operating qualities will probably be quite limited.

The mechanics of planning

Do not try to design the final plan on the first try. It is almost impossible to do! Each track plan in this book and in RAILROADS YOU CAN MODEL was the result of several tries and optimizations. Use tissue paper when sketching out track designs so you can trace over features you are satisfied with and want to keep when making subsequent designs. You can also use a photocopy machine.

In developing the actual track plan, do not start by drawing a diagram of your room unless it is very small—then you have to. With more moderate and large spaces, work out a general plan in rough sketch form first. This can be very loose. Try several.

Next, make a detailed plan of each important terminal and switching point on tracing paper. Do each on a separate sheet. Here is where you can use the track-planning template in the back of the book PRACTICAL GUIDE TO MODEL RAILROADING. You simply slide tracing paper over the template and trace switches, straight track, and curves of various radii as you wish. Use a compass to draw your minimum radius curves. Larger curves can be drawn freehand or with a French curve.

Now make a plan of your room space to the same scale as your detail plans. Show aisles with dashed lines, not solid. Slide the switching plans around in the spaces until you find an arrangement that looks workable and good.

Add connecting tracks, usually with long, sweeping curves rather than straight, and, finally, add industrial spurs to provide for plenty of places to deliver and pick up freight cars.

With the help of a copy machine, you can duplicate your switching sketches and try several other arrangements, taking only a few minutes for each trial.

There is no need to determine the exact location for switches and track routes, even when drawing what you feel will be your final track plan. Why? Because when you actually lay track, you will find that minor (and occasionally major) alterations will always be necessary. Many alterations become obvious only during actual construction and not on paper. The important point is that you have an overall idea of where things will go so you can begin putting track down and be on your way to running a railroad.

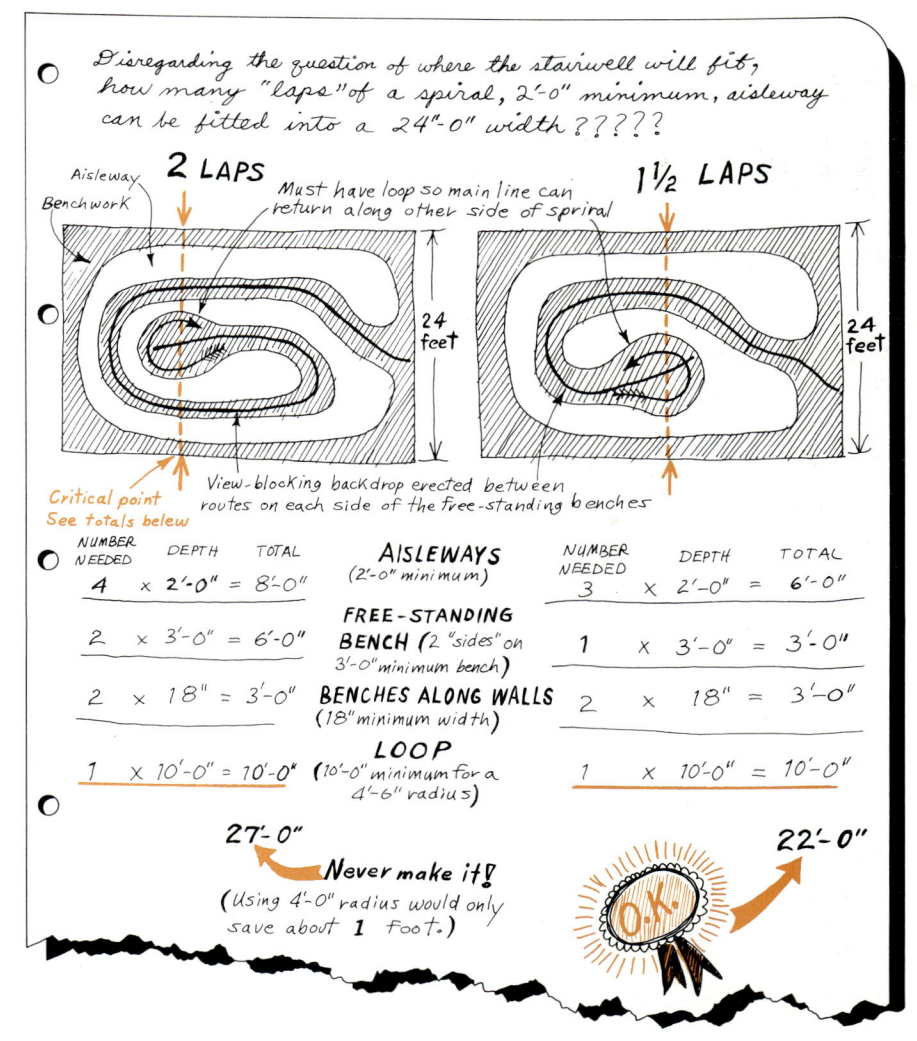

Start your track planning with general notes, sketches, and ideas, perhaps in a notebook. Here, noted track planner John Armstrong has been calculating aisle sizes for his layout space to figure out how much room he'll have left for track and scenery.

A splash of color — Monon's then-new red-and-two-tone-gray paint scheme on new EMD F3's — pervades the tranquil mood of the Indiana countryside as the southbound Day Express glides over Salt Creek near Harrodsburg. The date: June 10, 1947.

Monon

The modeling possibilities are fine all up and down the Hoosier Line

MONON ROUTE

MENTION Indiana railroads to a railfan and he probably will envision grain elevators and box cars, prairies and straight tracks, and tree-clad villages and towns with stately courthouses and rustic railroad depots, and . . . the Monon — "The Hoosier Line" — Indiana's own railroad.

The 541-mile Monon was merged into the 6048-mile Louisville & Nashville in 1971, ending what was perhaps the most colorful chapter in Indiana railroading history. The oddity of this Class I carrier was that all its track was within the state of Indiana. Monon trains reached into Kentucky (Louis-

Following a lofty crossing of the Ohio River on the K&IT bridge (which autos also use), northbound train 72 rumbles into New Albany, Ind. Note signal on tower.

TRAINS: Linn H. Westcott.

Monon's "pumpkin vine" line to coal fields branched from the main at lonely Wallace Junction. Facilities included car scales, water tower, coaling tower, and car-repair sheds. Train is northbound.

J. P. Lamb Jr.

Monon purchased nine of the 58 BL2's that EMD produced, numbering them 30-38. Monon intended them for freight service — here No. 33 works at Crawfordsville with a local in June 1958 — but occasionally they showed up in charge of passenger consists.

Gary W. Dolzall.

(Above) Alco Century 420 No. 504 leads three sister units and southbound train 73 across Clear Creek just south of Diamond, Ind., in July 1971. L&N merger was only days away. (Below) Post-merger evidence at Hammond in September 1971: Monon-scheme U23B and C420 are spliced by an L&N U25B.

TRAINS: J. David Ingles.

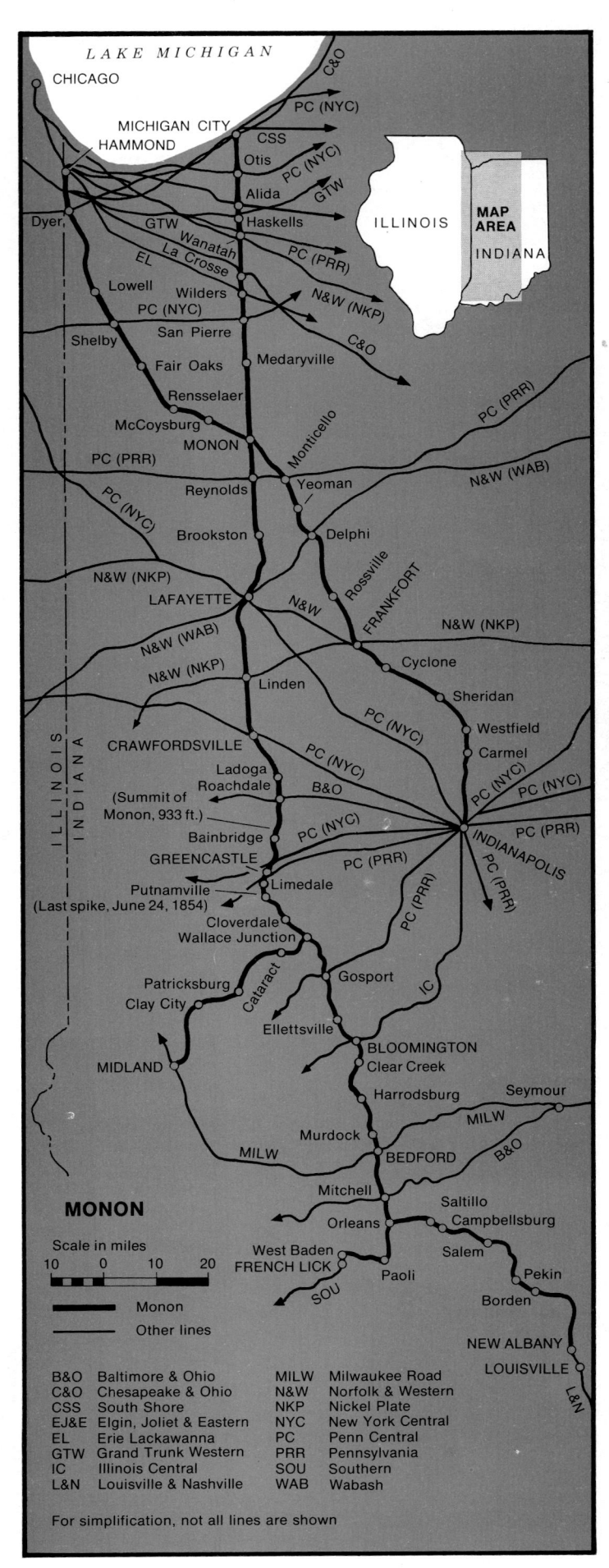

MONON

Scale in miles
10 0 10 20

— Monon
— Other lines

B&O	Baltimore & Ohio	MILW	Milwaukee Road
C&O	Chesapeake & Ohio	N&W	Norfolk & Western
CSS	South Shore	NKP	Nickel Plate
EJ&E	Elgin, Joliet & Eastern	NYC	New York Central
EL	Erie Lackawanna	PC	Penn Central
GTW	Grand Trunk Western	PRR	Pennsylvania
IC	Illinois Central	SOU	Southern
L&N	Louisville & Nashville	WAB	Wabash

For simplification, not all lines are shown

5

Class H-6 2-8-0 No. 286 was 31 years old in this 1942 photo at Sheridan. CI&L's seven 2-8-0's were numbered 280-286. *William A. Swartz.*

Engineer and Class G-2a 4-6-0 (built by CI&L early in the 1920's) pose at Lafayette in 1939. There were 24 4-6-0's. *Harold K. Vollrath: collection of Dennis Wozniczka.*

Largest steam power on the Hoosier Line: eight Class L-1 2-10-2's built by Alco in 1914-1916. They were numbered 600-607. *Harold K. Vollrath: collection of Dennis Wozniczka.*

Monon's 4-6-2's — the K class — were the mainstay of steam-era passenger power. K-5a No. 444 (Alco, 1923) pauses southbound at Wanatah on the Michigan City branch in 1946 with an inspection train. Monon crossed PRR's Chicago-Pittsburgh main line here. *TRAINS: Linn H. Westcott.*

Monon owned two Atlantics, Class I-1a, Nos. 390 and 391. Brooks built them in 1901. *CI&L.*

ville) and Illinois (Chicago) by trackage rights. The Monon truly was the Hoosier State's own railroad.

Monon's ancestry goes back to the Albany & Salem Railroad, organized in July 1847. In those days New Albany was the largest city in Indiana. In fact, New Albanites scoffed at talk that Louisville, on the opposite shore of the Ohio River, eventually might eclipse New Albany in importance. Michigan City, on the shores of Lake Michigan 287 miles north of New Albany, was in the same position — it feared Chicago no more than New Albany feared Louisville, and was confident it would become a great port. The New Albany & Salem was projected to connect these two great-cities-to-be. The two population centers were linked in 1854, and the first through train between Michigan City and New Albany operated on July 3rd of that year.

The completion of the Indianapolis & St. Louis (later part of the Big Four Route) between Indianapolis and Terre Haute, crossing the NA&S at Greencastle, provided a new through route for freight bound from Cincinnati and the East to Chicago: I&StL handled the freight between Indianapolis and Greencastle, NA&S relayed it to Michigan City, and Michigan Central took it to Chicago.

In 1859 the NA&S was renamed Louisville, New Albany & Chicago. The Kentucky & Indiana Bridge had been completed and trains were running *through* New Albany into Louisville. Unfortunately for the LNA&C, the Big Four had constructed its own route to Chicago (via Kankakee, Ill., and the Illinois Central Railroad), diverting a substantial amount of traffic from the LNA&C. LNA&C began studying the possibility of extending its own track to Chicago; the chartering of the Chicago & Indianapolis Air Line Railway was the first step. The C&IAL planned to construct the shortest possible railroad route between its namesake cities. In 1880 the line extended from Delphi to Dyer, Ind., crossing the LNA&C at Monon, named after nearby Monon Creek (Monon is a Potawatomi Indian word meaning "swift running"). In 1881 the Air Line was merged into LNA&C and the line was completed between Dyer and Hammond, and between Delphi and Indianapolis. By the early 1900's the LNA&C's few branches had been formed, usually through acquisition of smaller railroads. In 1897 the LNA&C was reorganized as the Chicago, Indianapolis & Louisville — nicknamed the Monon Route.

The CI&L entered a period of relative prosperity after the turn of the century, but went bankrupt in 1933. The road managed to creak along until 1946 when John W. Barriger III became president of the Monon Route. Barriger rebuilt the Monon completely, dieselizing the road, purchasing more than 1000 new freight cars (and scrapping nearly 1200 old ones), and relocating the line to eliminate grades steeper than .5 per

6

cent and curves sharper than 2 degrees. During the Barriger years the Monon became a highly respected, well-organized, progressive railroad. In 1956 the railroad adopted its popular nickname, Monon, as its official title.

The Monon is a fine choice for modeling because it has so much to offer. It was a compact freight and passenger carrier with a single-track main line, branch lines, and pusher grades. The post-1946 Monon was a study of contrasts — a progressive railroad in a bucolic setting of green farmlands and tranquil Hoosier towns.

Monon's livelihood

Most of Monon's freight business was bridge traffic, but a large amount of tonnage, mostly coal and Bedford limestone, originated on-line. Monon also carried a great deal of gravel, cement, lumber, minerals, and agricultural products. Coal came from strip mines near Clay City and Midland on the I&L branch (formerly the Indianapolis & Louisville Railway) to Victoria. Stone was quarried near Bloomington and Bedford, and much of the cement came from Limedale and Mitchell. Gosport originated many carloads of gravel.

Principal connections for interchange traffic were the Elgin, Joliet & Eastern at Dyer and most lines west and north out of Chicago; the Southern and the Louisville & Nashville at Louisville; Milwaukee Road at Bedford and Midland; the New York Central (former Big Four, later Penn Central) at several places; Nickel Plate (later Norfolk & Western) at South Wanatah, Lafayette, Linden, Frankfort, and Indianapolis; and the Baltimore & Ohio at Mitchell, Roachdale, Alida, Louisville, and Indianapolis. Of course, the Monon-Michigan City line intersected most rail lines radiating eastward from Chicago.

In the early 1880's Monon offered through passenger service to Cincinnati with the *Velvet Train* and the *Electric* (named for the newest kind of power in the land) operated jointly with the Cincinnati, Hamilton & Dayton via Indianapolis. In 1911 the *Hoosier Limited* was introduced between Chicago and French Lick, Ind., site of famous French Lick Springs Hotel. In conjunction with the Monon, through sleeping cars from the Pennsylvania, NYC, and B&O were operated to the famous health spa. The principal passenger route of the Monon was the Chicago-Indianapolis line, sporting such trains as the *Hoosier, Tippecanoe*, and the *Mid-Night Special*.

Patronage declined in the 1950's and 1960's, until finally Monon's last passenger train, the Chicago-Louisville *Thoroughbred*, was discontinued in 1967. Monon often operated special passenger trains to football games at on-line universities and to the Kentucky Derby in Louisville, even after regular passenger service was dropped in 1967.

Two photos, TRAINS: Linn H. Westcott.

Industries such as this lumber mill (above left) at Greencastle help to give a model railroad purpose by simulating traffic generation. (Above right) A model Monon should include stone industries if the southern portion of the railroad is represented. Oolitic limestone is cut from the ground in large blocks at a quarry and moved by a local freight called a "stone train" to nearby mills. The blocks are cut into building stone of various sizes and shapes, reloaded into freight cars using overhead cranes (below), and shipped all over the country. The mill pictured is at Bloomington.

KALMBACH BOOKS: Harold A. Edmonson.

Equipment

Brooks, Baldwin, Rogers, and Alco built steam power for the Monon, and Monon itself constructed steam locomotives during the 1920's. Alco built most of Monon's steam power, and even a number of Monon diesels during the 1960's. The mainstay of the steam-era was a fleet of Alco-built Class J 2-8-2's delivered between 1912 and 1929.

Twenty-four Alco Class K 4-6-2's and a sprinkling of Atlantics provided power for Monon passenger flagships. Overall, Monon had no truly powerful steam power because of load limits, nor could any of the power be considered modern. Unfortunately, even the latest of the Mikado-type freight haulers, the series of Class J's delivered in 1929, could not be considered modern because the engines were ordered on a cost basis, not on the basis of what the railroad needed. By the time dieselization rolled around, most CI&L steam power was ready for the scrapyard.

John F. Humiston.

In 1947 Monon bought nine Alco RS2's, Nos. 21-29 (51-59 after Shops rebuilt them in the 1960's), for freight and passenger duties. No. 26 is at Michigan City with a 1948 railfan special.

Marre-Mott collection: J. David Ingles.

Back-to-back C628's tow northbound freight (and two Savannah & Atlanta switchers) through Dyer, Ind., in 1965. All Monon 628's, Nos. 400-408, were traded in on C420's in 1967.

P. F. Johnson.

FM H15-44's Nos. 36 and 37 arrived in 1947. They were renumbered 45 and 46 when BL2's 36-38 were delivered in 1949.

J. P. Lamb Jr.

(Above) A sparse load of passengers awaits the southbound Thoroughbred at Monon on April 4, 1959. The brick building at left is the Monon House Hotel. Monon depot fronted the Indianapolis line. (Left) Street running was a Monon tradition, and modelers will note many details in this 1947 Lafayette street scene showing the northbound Day Express. Thirty-one years later, passenger trains (albeit Amtrak, not Monon) still coasted down 5th Street, but the stately Lafayette depot had become an antique store.

TRAINS: W. A. Akin Jr.

Mini modeling project: concrete overpass.

M. D. McCarter.

Monon acquired its first diesels in 1942 — three EMD (Electro-Motive Division, General Motors) NW2's and one EMD SW1 — but not until John Barriger came to the Monon did the CI&L project a plan for complete dieselization. By the end of 1948 all steam was gone from the Monon. By the end of 1949 Monon had a handsome fleet of diesels: 30 EMD F3's had conquered the domain of the 2-8-2's and 4-6-2's in general freight and passenger service; four additional NW2's, nine EMD BL2's, nine Alco RS2's, and one H10-44 and two H15-44's built by Fairbanks-Morse handled switching and local-freight duties. The H15-44's frequented the limestone quarry branches in the Bloomington-Bedford area, primarily the quarries at Murdock. Although intended for freight service, several of the RS2's were equipped with steam generators for passenger service. Diesel fans were attracted to the Monon because of its long-lived BL2's, oddities in EMD's catalog of standardization.

In the 1960's and in 1970, Monon bought second-generation diesels from Alco and General Electric. The locomotives that had dieselized the Monon in the late 1940's had put in many years of useful service, and their replacement was necessary. Nine Century 628's built by Alco joined the Monon roster in 1964, followed by 18 Century 420's in 1966-1967. The big six-axle, six-motor C628's proved to be too heavy for Monon's trackage, and were traded in on some of the C420's in 1967. Two 420's which were equipped with steam generators replaced RS2's and F3's used on the Chicago-Louisville *Thoroughbred*, Monon's last remaining passenger train. After Alco ceased building locomotives in 1969, Monon turned to General Electric for new diesels — eight U23B's delivered in 1970 just prior to merger with the L&N.

Although some diesels appeared in an early CI&L paint scheme, most Monon diesels eventually wore a black-and-gold livery representing the colors of Purdue University in Lafayette. Ten passenger F3's sported a striking paint scheme of red and gray with white striping (supposedly representing the cream-and-crimson colors of Indiana University in Bloomington), but these later were repainted black and gold.

When Monon purchased hundreds of new freight cars under Barriger's direction, the railroad applied a radical, although logical, system of numbering to the new equipment: The cars were numbered from 1 on — no five-digit numbers like those found on most railroads. Boxcar numbers started at 1 and ran to 1690, with some omissions (30 coke cars were numbered 1000 to 1029). Tank cars were numbered in the 1800's; gondolas, 3001 to 3850 and 4725 to 4999; hoppers, 4001 to 4600; ballast cars, 5001 to 5020; flat cars, 7000 to 7510. Another series of box cars started in the 9000's. Only some of the older gondolas and hoppers retained five-digit numbers. (Needless to say, Monon box car No. 1 became a celebrity as train watchers all around the country took note of its travels.)

From the time Pullman delivered the famous five-car *Velvet Train* to the Monon in 1889, to the warm September day in 1967 on which the *Thoroughbred* made its last run to Chicago, Monon passenger trains occupied a warm spot in the hearts of Hoosiers. Early passenger cars — products of Ohio Falls Car Manufacturing (which later became American Car & Foundry) and Pullman — clicked off the miles between Chicago, Indianapolis, Louisville, and French Lick. Monon passenger traffic reached its nadir in the years immediately following World War II, when CI&L was down to a single train a day between Chicago and Louisville, with a connection for Indianapolis at Monon.

When Barriger came to the Monon in 1946, the newest passenger car on the system dated from 1923. Barriger wanted new streamlined equipment placed into service on expanded passenger schedules as soon as possible, but carbuilders were already so busy working on orders for new streamliners for other railroads that cars for the Monon couldn't be delivered until at least 1948. Barriger did not want to wait, so the railroad purchased 34 secondhand semi-streamlined U. S. Army hospital cars and transformed them into beautiful red-and-gray parlor cars, diner-lounges, coaches, and other types of cars

CI&L.
Traveling celebrity: Train-watchers made it a point to look for Monon box car 1.

CI&L.
Monon introduced this well-remembered freight-car scheme early in the 1950's. "The Hoosier Line" lettering was black on a gray letterboard; remainder of car was boxcar red with white lettering.

G. W. Hockaday.
Monon's welded-steel cabooses had extended-vision cupolas, rounded windows.

TRAINS: Linn H. Westcott.
Hospital car-turned-coach wore two shades of gray, "Monon Royal Red" (window band, letters, herald field), black (roof), and white (stripes, numbers, herald).

for use on new Monon streamliners, the *Hoosier, Tippecanoe, Varsity, Bluegrass,* and *Thoroughbred*. Some old baggage cars, RPO-baggage cars, standard sleepers, and troop sleepers converted to express cars were used on Monon streamliners, but these were repainted from Pullman green to red-and-gray to match the new passenger equipment. Eventually most Monon passenger equipment was repainted black and gold.

Geography and physical plant

The northern part of Indiana is generally flat throughout Monon territory, especially on the Monon-Michigan City branch. This line is absolutely straight from Westville, just south of Michigan City, to Brookston, 15 miles south of Monon — 64.52 miles without a curve, one of the longest stretches of straight track in the country. Try modeling that in your basement! (Incidentally, you would need a basement nearly 3900 feet long to model this stretch of track exactly in HO scale.)

The Monon main line headed due south from Hammond to Dyer before turning eastward, crossing a plain which once formed the bottom of a larger Lake Michigan during glacial times. The plain comes to an abrupt end between Dyer and St. John. Moraines deposited by ancient glaciers form a ridge of low hills that force every railroad entering Chicago from the east to take on easy curves and climb gentle grades. As it neared Lafayette, the main line dropped into the Wabash River valley on a 1 per cent grade, steep enough to have required pushers on some trains northbound out of Lafayette during the days of steam. Below Lafayette the line entered some rolling country. (Actually, "rolling country" is a modest description for some parts of Indiana.) South from Lafayette the line climbed gradually for 50 miles to a high point near Bainbridge, crossing several valleys en route. The next 150 miles to Louisville were just one dive after another, giving the Monon a sawtooth profile. The Monon was a cross-drainage route. All the way from Hammond to Indianapolis and Louisville the line crossed one river after another, and climbed the ridges in between. Between Bloomington and Harrodsburg the Monon crossed Clear Creek 14 times in 10 miles! Many hills along the line required some steam-powered freight trains to double; that is, the trains had to be divided in two and taken over the hill one section at a time.

The grades which required steam-powered freight trains to double were located at Delphi southward and northward where the Indianapolis line crossed the Wabash River; at Gosport, southward and northward crossing the White River; southward and northward to Bedford; northward at Salem; and northward from Borden to Pekin. Pusher grades were north out of the Wabash River valley from Lafayette to Battle Ground, and north out of Bloomington (the latter remained a pusher grade into dieselization; in fact, some L&N trains still require pushers on the grade).

The Monon was divided into the Northern and Southern divisions. Lafayette (Shops) was the main division point, and all dispatching was done from there.

9

The only Monon-owned interlocking tower was at Clay City where the Midland branch intersected the Big Four (NYC).

Picturesque frame stations enhanced Monon's "storyland" setting. Weathered Cloverdale depot has three types of siding.

Wilson's milk plant at Sheridan in the 1940's. Milk was an important commodity for many railroads before the 1960's.

Monon's principal yards were located in Hammond, Michigan City, Monon, Lafayette, Bloomington, and Indianapolis. Monon transfer freights moved cars from South Hammond yard to Chicago's huge Clearing Yard in southwest suburban Chicago. From South Hammond yard the Monon main line extended north through downtown Hammond to the junction with the Chicago & Western Indiana Railroad at State Line tower on the Indiana-Illinois border. Monon trains operated over C&WI trackage between State Line and Chicago; Monon passenger trains used Dearborn Station in downtown Chicago.

Modest yard and engine facilities were maintained at Michigan City and Indianapolis; in later days these two lines were considered branches, and trains usually only made "turns" to these cities. Passenger trains on the Second Subdivision entered Indianapolis Union Station via the Nickel Plate and the Big Four.

Lafayette, the largest city between Chicago and Louisville on the Monon, was the Monon "capital," because it was the location of the railroad's shops and general offices. At Shops (official designation for Monon's yard and shop area in Lafayette) at the north end of town were the engine terminal and a yard, locomotive repair facilities, company warehouses, supply stores, motive-power offices, and a roundhouse (dismantled in the late 1940's). The importance of Lafayette Shops diminished after Monon's merger with L&N. Monon's general offices were located at the end of Fifth Street, and it was at this point (and still is for the L&N) that Fifth Street became the right of way for the main line for over a mile through downtown Lafayette. Near downtown the track passes what was once Monon's passenger station, a stately structure built of Bedford limestone. In later years, Monon passenger trains stopped at a new station adjacent to the company offices to avoid tying up traffic on Fifth Street. Ironically, after Amtrak's Chicago-Florida trains began using the former Monon route through Indiana in 1975, a downtown Lafayette station stop was reinstated, but at the Lahr Hotel rather than the original Monon depot.

Lafayette is not the only town in which Monon invaded the streets. In Bedford the Monon passed right through downtown on one of the main streets beside the courthouse square, and in New Albany most street running is in a residential area. Traffic lights in Lafayette, Bedford, and New Albany still line up green for L&N trains rumbling through town. The Monon

(Left) A five-car Indianapolis-bound Tippecanoe approaches Monticello's board-and-batten depot on a Christmas-picture day in December 1950. Mother Nature was not a Monon fan: A tornado leveled the station 24 years later. (Below left) Mainstay of steam freight power were 55 Class J 2-8-2's. J-4 No. 571 thunders past Limedale tower near Greencastle with northbound tonnage in August 1946. (Below) Through sleepers from different regions of the U. S. brought tourists to French Lick Springs Hotel; sleeper setout tracks were in close proximity to hotel entrance. Regular through-car service (via the Bluegrass out of Chicago) to the resort ended in 1949.

10

also had some street operation in Monticello and Frankfort.

McDoel Yard at Bloomington contained repair, classification, fueling, and servicing facilities. At McDoel trains were adjusted in length because of the difference in grades north and south of town. Also at McDoel, sleepers bound for French Lick were separated from mainline Chicago-Louisville trains and relayed south to French Lick Springs Hotel as a separate train.

Monon trains reached Kentucky & Indiana Terminal's Youngtown Yard in Louisville by crossing the Ohio River on K&IT's mammoth railroad and highway bridge. Southern and Baltimore & Ohio freight trains also used Youngtown Yard. The K&IT, partly owned by Monon, performed switching and transfer duties in the Louisville area and had (and still has) a substantial yard and engine terminal, although Monon Division L&N trains today bypass Youngtown and use L&N's Strawberry Yard in South Louisville.

With numerous limestone quarries on its lines, it's not surprising that many Monon depots were constructed of Bedford limestone. Bedford limestone stations could be found at Lafayette, Bloomington, Monon, French Lick, and (of course) Bedford. Unfortunately, the handsome limestone depot at Monon was knocked down many years ago when a runaway *Thoroughbred* derailed into it. It was replaced with a modern brick building. Some depots along the Hoosier Line were of board-and-batten construction, such as at Greencastle, Wanatah, and Monticello, and many others were brick. The depots at Michigan City, Orleans, and Gosport were unusual in that they had run-through freight tracks; freight cars could be pushed right into the station for loading and unloading.

Monon vaulted over rivers and valleys on some impressive bridges, notably at Monticello over the Tippecanoe River, at Delphi over the Wabash River, and near Paoli on the French Lick branch.

Designing a track plan

At first glance the Monon track plan may appear to be that of a "dream layout," but when built in N scale the layout can fit into a space about 14 feet wide and 22 feet long if two sides are butted against the walls. We designed the plan with N scale in mind because of the large amount of operation you can pack into a relatively small area, but as with all the plans in the book the plan can be built in other scales by modifying the size of the aisleways.

We completed three Monon track plans (and started many more) before deciding on the one that appears in this chapter. We stumbled into the usual pitfalls of layout planning with our initial attempts. In our first plan we tried to cram too much into a given space. Just about all Monon lines were represented, but the layout would have been a spaghetti-like arrangement of tracks with too many route options — not a good base for operation. As track plans go, our second effort had excellent operating possibilities, but we had left out too many prototype features that radiated Monon charisma. You might say we over-selective compressionized!

By the time we had started the third plan, a Monon afficionado had joined the ranks of Kalmbach employees, so we

Monon's main line ran close to downtown Bloomington. Note the courthouse in this 1947 scene of No. 74 nearing the depot.

Gosport, Orleans, and (pictured) Michigan City had rare, run-through depots.

Seven EMD NW2's, Nos. 11-17 delivered in the 1940's, held down most switching chores. No. 16 is at South Hammond.

If you model Greencastle, include the Monon Grill near the station so the local-freight crew can have a place to go for lunch.

Business car-equipped inspection train holds on Bedford siding as the southbound Day Express takes on passengers. Beyond depot, tracks take to the street. Year: 1946.

11

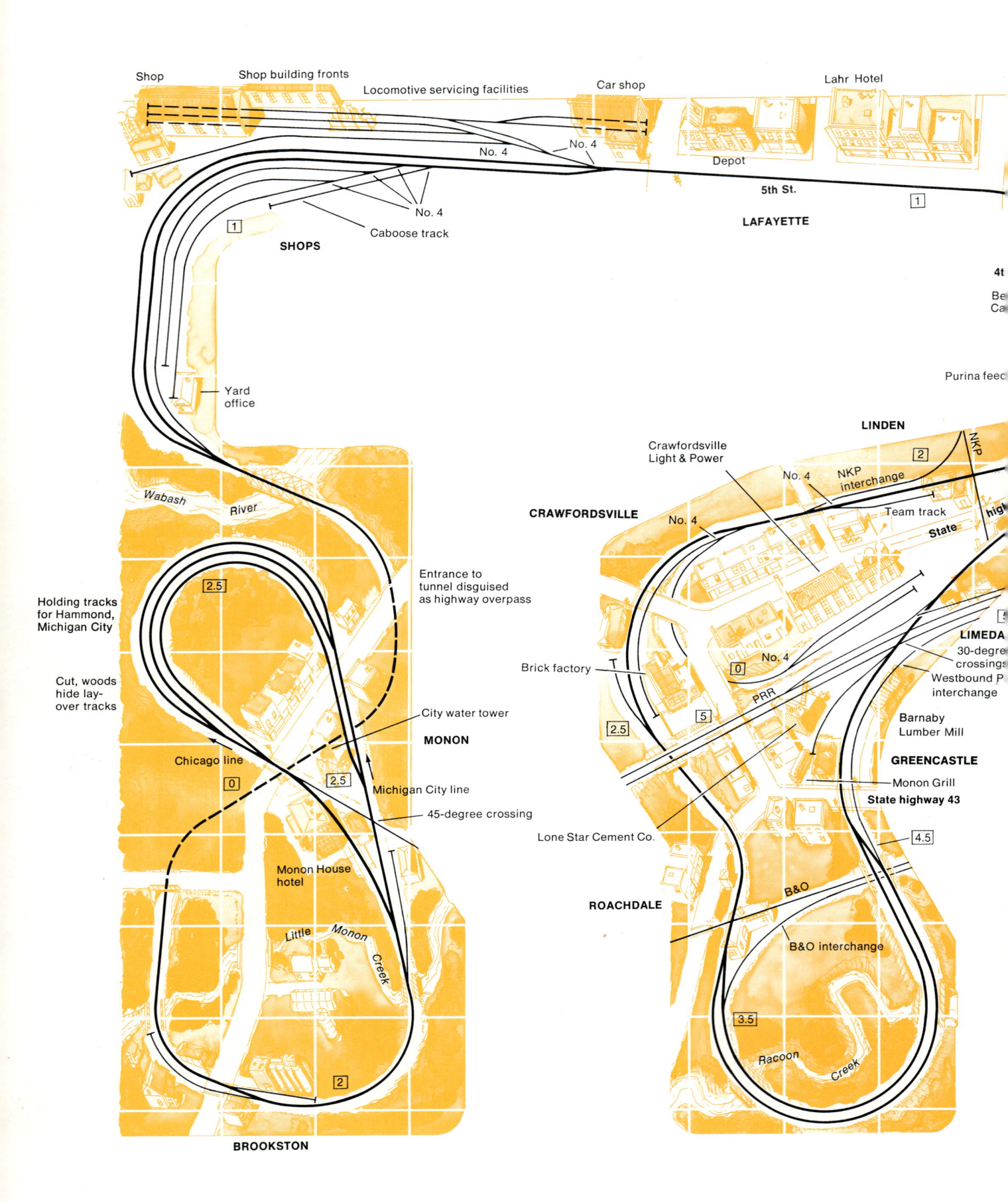

Shop   Shop building fronts   Locomotive servicing facilities   Car shop   Lahr Hotel

Depot

No. 4   No. 4

5th St.   [1]

No. 4   LAFAYETTE

Caboose track

[1]

SHOPS   4t

Be
Ca

Purina feed

Yard office

LINDEN

Crawfordsville Light & Power   [2]   NKP

No. 4   NKP interchange

Wabash River   CRAWFORDSVILLE   No. 4   Team track

State   high

Entrance to tunnel disguised as highway overpass

[2.5]

LIMEDA

Holding tracks for Hammond, Michigan City   No. 4   30-degree crossings

Brick factory   Westbound P interchange

Cut, woods hide lay-over tracks   [0]   Barnaby Lumber Mill

City water tower   PRR   GREENCASTLE

MONON   [5]

Chicago line   [2.5]   Monon Grill

[0]   [2.5]   State highway 43

Michigan City line

45-degree crossing   Lone Star Cement Co.   [4.5]

Monon House hotel   ROACHDALE   B&O

Little Monon Creek   B&O interchange

[2]   [3.5]

Racoon Creek

BROOKSTON

12

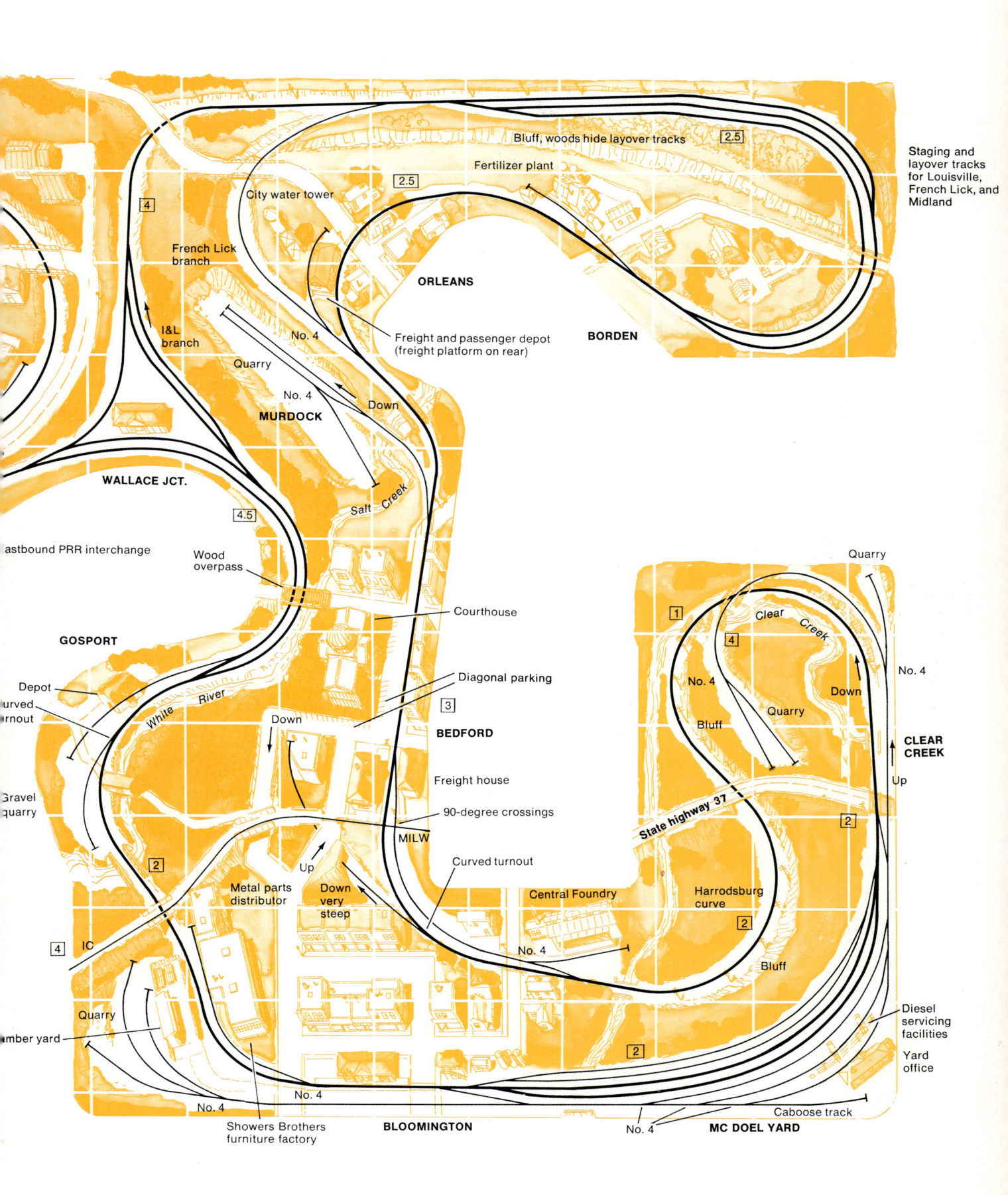

Staging and layover tracks for Louisville, French Lick, and Midland

Bluff, woods hide layover tracks
[2.5]
Fertilizer plant
[2.5]
City water tower
[4]
French Lick branch
I&L branch
ORLEANS
BORDEN
Freight and passenger depot (freight platform on rear)
No. 4
Quarry
No. 4
Down
MURDOCK
Salt Creek
WALLACE JCT.
[4.5]
Eastbound PRR interchange
Wood overpass
Courthouse
GOSPORT
Depot
Curved turnout
White River
Diagonal parking
[3]
BEDFORD
Down
Freight house
90-degree crossings
MILW
Gravel quarry
Up
Curved turnout
Quarry
Clear Creek
[1]
No. 4
[4]
Down
Bluff
Quarry
No. 4
CLEAR CREEK
Up
State highway 37
[2]
Metal parts distributor
Down very steep
Central Foundry
Harrodsburg curve
[2]
Bluff
[2]
[4] IC
Quarry
Lumber yard
No. 4
Diesel servicing facilities
Yard office
[2]
No. 4
No. 4
Showers Brothers furniture factory
BLOOMINGTON
No. 4
MC DOEL YARD
Caboose track

13

Exhaust rustles the leaves as two RS2's hustle the Bloomington-to-Louisville local through a curve near Guthrie, Ind., in 1971.
Gary W. Dolzall.

While the crew "goes for beans," Class E-1b 4-8-0 No. 230 rests in Michigan City in 1946. Twenty-two 4-8-0's comprised the E class.
P. F. Johnson.

asked him to list those prototype Monon features that should be modeled to capture the flavor of the Hoosier Line. He recommended that the layout have several short stone quarry branches, street running, the I&L coal branch (or at least Wallace Junction), the town of Monon, the yards at Lafayette and Bloomington, a major interchange with a major east-west rail line (we settled on the PRR at Limedale, although other interchanges are represented), Gosport's famous "run-through" depot, and at least one grain elevator town on the north end of the layout. Back to the drawing board.

Next question. On what basic operational schematic should we base the track plan? Bruce Chubb's HOW TO OPERATE YOUR MODEL RAILROAD gave us some insight here. We decided to use a loop-to-loop scheme with layover tracks at the loops and intermediate yards. We also opted for a walk-in-type layout with a progressive track route so that operators could follow their trains (using walkaround throttles) from one end of the run to the other without ducking under benchwork. It is impractical to model a railroad in its entirety, even a smaller company, so we concentrated on modeling the Monon main line between Monon and Borden, Ind., and leaving other mainline and branch operations mostly to the imagination.

Up and down the (model) Monon line

The best way to see the layout is to take an imaginary cab ride on our model of the Monon. The southbound *Thoroughbred* should give us a good view of the line; we'll "board" at Monon as soon as the train arrives from "Chicago" (actually some hidden layover tracks just beyond Monon). A red-and-gray EMD F3 trailed by several passenger cars rolls into the depot. Departure time comes, and the engineer gives two blasts on the air horn and notches out on the throttle. The V16 behind our backs revs up with the familiar EMD chant, and we begin to move. We cross over Little Monon Creek and swing through Brookston, a town typical of flat, agricultural (the grain elevator is the clue) northern Indiana. Next stop is Lafayette. Once past the yard and shops our train enters street trackage and pauses briefly for passengers at the depot. The prototype depot stood on the west side of the street, but because there is no west side of the street at this point, we have used modeler's license to locate the station on the east side. Traffic respects our movement through Lafayette's city streets, and shortly we find ourselves out in the countryside.

At Linden, Monon interchanges freight with the New York, Chicago & St. Louis (Nickel Plate), but our passenger train is not scheduled to stop here. We do stop for passengers at Crawfordsville though, and not too far from the station we catch a glimpse of the Crawfordsville Light & Power Company. Our model Monon services this plant via a spur off the main line just north of the station. Many of the coal-laden hoppers that come off the I&L branch are destined to this power plant. Our train soon resumes its southbound journey.

We make a brief stop at Roachdale, primarily a freight interchange point with Baltimore & Ohio's Indianapolis-Springfield (Ill.) line, and curve into the rolling countryside before gliding to a stop in front of the Greencastle station. Limedale is nearby. A heavy amount of interchange is carried out at Limedale, where dummy tracks representing Pennsylvania's double-track St. Louis-Pittsburgh main line crosses the Monon. Cement-related industries are located in Limedale.

Beyond Limedale we coast through Wallace Junction, where the I&L coal branch takes off to our left. If we were to model the prototype Wallace Junction exactly, the branch would go off from our right, but then the real Monon wasn't confined to a basement. Our train rolls through bucolic Gosport next to the White River, one of the prettiest spots on the line, and then ducks under

Scale modeled		Z	N	TT	HO	S	O
Spacing of rulings	in.	9.00	12.00	18.00	24.00	36.00	48.00
Space horizontally	ft.-in.	19-0	19-6	26-3	33-0	49-5	65-11
Space vertically	ft.-in.	11-0	11-3	15-10	20-6	30-8	40-11
Minimum radius, main line	in.	9.00	12.00	18.00	24.00	36.00	48.00
Minimum radius, secondary tracks	in.	7.00	9.00	13.50	18.00	27.00	36.00
Parallel straight track spacing	in.	.63	.95	1.27	1.75	2.38	3.17
Parallel curved track spacing	in.	1.00	1.50	1.99	2.75	3.74	4.98
Multiply elevations by	in.	.66	1.00	1.33	1.83	2.49	3.32
Turnouts: Unless otherwise indicated, No. 6 in all scales							
Spacing of rulings	mm.	225.00	300.00	450.00	600.00	900.00	1200.00
Space horizontally	m.	4.83	5.84	7.87	9.89	14.83	19.78
Space vertically	m.	2.68	3.37	4.75	6.14	9.21	12.28
Minimum radius, main line	mm.	225.00	300.00	450.00	600.00	900.00	1200.00
Minimum radius, secondary tracks	mm.	169.00	225.00	338.00	450.00	675.00	900.00
Parallel straight track spacing	mm.	17.00	24.00	32.00	44.00	59.00	79.00
Parallel curved track spacing	mm.	27.00	37.00	50.00	69.00	93.00	125.00
Multiply elevations by	mm.	18.00	25.00	33.00	46.00	62.00	83.00

Horizontal and vertical dimensions of this layout allow for a minimum aisleway width of 24" (60 cm.). To maintain this minimum aisleway width when using Z scale, the layout should be expanded at the suggested locations indicated by dashed lines.

So that all areas of a model railroad remain accessible, no portion of a layout should be more than 30" (75 cm.) from an aisleway or access opening. Thus, when constructing a layout to the Monon track-plan dimensions in a scale larger than N, it may be necessary to add access openings or lift-out scenery sections where not already shown.

the Illinois Central's Mattoon (Ill.)-Indianapolis line (another dummy track to help separate different areas of scenery). Off to our right we see some stone quarry branches and on the left, the Showers Brothers furniture factory. We're entering Bloomington and in moments our train rolls to a stop in front of Bloomington's handsome oolitic limestone station. Bloomington is home of Indiana University, so we imagine that a large number of passengers are detraining here. We ease out of the station and then make a short stop at the yard office at McDoel to simulate the changing of crews and to drop off a coach.

We leave McDoel and slip past the small frame structure that serves as the Clear Creek depot, and on our right we see another quarry branch. Stone was one of the most important traffic sources on the real Monon, so it's only natural that we represent that source on our model. The branch ascends and crosses over the main line just before we cross Clear Creek for the second time since leaving Bloomington. While in the Clear Creek valley, our train drifts around famous Harrodsburg curve, a location for many Monon publicity photos.

We clatter across Milwaukee Road's Seymour (Ind.) branch just before coming to a stop in front of Bedford station (also of limestone construction). Beyond the station we see that we have to fight city traffic again. Our F3 is big enough to send Fords and Chevys scurrying for the curb, but we have to watch for double-parked trucks. Those side-mounted rearview mirrors can leave a scar the length of our train.

Murdock is just beyond Bedford. In reality Murdock, another important quarry location, is north of Bedford, but we have moved it to the south side of town to make room for Harrodsburg curve. During our stop at Orleans we note the French Lick line branching off from our left (again, for reasons of space, we've flopped the prototype track arrangement to fit our requirements). In moments we pull out for Louisville, which is merely one of the vacant tracks in the hidden storage loop.

More plan notes

The staging-track-within-a-loop arrangement at either end of the line permits us to imitate some of the prototype's operating patterns, as we'll see shortly. Although not feasible for steam operation, a train can leave either loop the same way it entered if the locomotives are run around the train. Or, a train can continue around the loop to re-emerge on the layout as a "different" train from a different line. For example, a northbound train can proceed through Monon as though it were headed for Chicago, pull into one of the layover tracks, and, after a specified layover time (if any), pull out of the loop and into Monon from "Michigan City."

One of the challenges to modeling Midwestern geography is that we can't always rely on mountains and tunnels to make our track route seem longer. Fortunately, southern Indiana terrain is more rugged than many people realize, so in modeling the Monon south of Greencastle we can employ deep cuts, bluffs, and twisting track. On other parts of the layout, however, we rely on city scenes and dummy intersecting rail lines for transition from one area to another.

We have used some sleight-of-hand scenery techniques to make some cities seem larger than they really are. The city scene backdrop routine works for Lafayette, but here's what we did for some of the other towns:

Certain cities on the layout have been combined to make them seem larger, but they have been strategically located so that viewers will not be aware that they are looking at more than one city. For example, Bedford and Bloomington constitute, basically, one urban area on the layout, but when a viewer faces Bloomington he will be unaware that he is also looking at a portion of Bedford— it will appear to be one big city. The same principle works for Bedford. We have also used this one-for-two technique at Greencastle and Crawfordsville.

We confess that we had to resort to having one tunnel on the line (under Monon), and in northern flatland Indiana on top of that! We suggest disguising the tunnel by placing highway overpasses at the tunnel mouths. Appropriately placed clusters of trees will also help.

By not completely hiding the loop layover tracks you'll avoid the how-do-I-hide-this-tunnel problem. Instead, locate the layover loops in deep cuts camouflaged by woods. There's no problem in letting the entrance tracks to the loops show. We can imagine them to be yard or passing-siding entrances. The important thing is not to be able to see all of either loop from any given vantage point.

Of course, you don't have to follow our Monon plan (or any plan in this book) track for track. If space is a problem, cut down the size of (or eliminate) one of the intermediate yards. (Better to do this than to cut down the number of industrial spurs; spurs are important for good operation.) Or, end the line at Bloomington and make the layout a point-to-loop run. The important thing is that the layout meets your own criteria for owning and operating an enjoyable model railroad.

The southbound Tippecanoe crosses its namesake river at Monticello in April 1959. No. 11's short consist is an ideal prototype for a pike-size passenger train.

The Thoroughbred departs for Chicago in 1963, leaving behind Louisville Union Station and L&N mail train No. 4. A single F3 (rebuilt following a wreck — note F7-type grilles) powers a consist that includes an express car rebuilt from a troop sleeper.

Shay 1925 works the Southern interchange at Topton, N. C., on May 27, 1975—the day before operations ceased on the Graham County. *Louis Saillard*

Graham County Railroad

The 12-mile Graham County Railroad served one town and ended nowhere. The prototype had fewer than 20 turnouts, some geared steam locomotives, a diesel, and a few cars

One can almost feel the heat of summer in this 1961 scene at Topton. The Southern train, with a Geep and an F, has just arrived to make setouts and pickups while the GC waits patiently at right. *Mallory Hope Ferrell.*

Shay 1926 struggles up the 5 per cent climb out of Topton in January 1963 with empty wood-chip cars bound for Bemis Lumber Co. in Robbinsville. The 1926 was purchased third hand in 1940. *Steve Patterson.*

NORTH CAROLINA has just about everything to offer the railroad modeler and fan. Besides the mountainous main lines and flatland speedways of the Class I carriers, the state has a large number of short lines. Perhaps the most special treat was the Graham County Railroad and its Bear Creek Scenic Railroad passenger operation where you had your choice of a 70-ton diesel or real steam-spitting Shay locomotives.

Along its snakelike trackage the short GC trains played hopscotch with Tulula Creek for most of the 12-mile (almost all of it upgrade) journey from Robbinsville to the junction with the Southern near Topton. The trains crossed the creek so often that a rider would lose count. Finally, the junction-bound train burst out of little Tulula Gap upon a scene of incredible splendor: spectacular Nantahala Gorge, carved for miles

16

Shay 1925 and loaded pulpwood cars sandwich a numberless, weathered ex-Southern caboose during switching maneuvers at the Bemis mill in July 1970. GC had several ex-SR cabooses on the property. Note such modeling details as the guardrail curve and the rails nearly covered by mud at the road crossing.

Robert L. Hogan.

March 1975 brought storms that washed out bridges between Bear Creek and Robbinsville, requiring GC to cut service back to Bear Creek. Shay 1925, the "Ed Collins" (named for her most devoted engineer), waits at Bear Creek on May 27, 1975, for furniture from Robbinsville to be transferred to box cars.

Daniel F. Watson Jr.

below and to the east of the Red Marble Gap area. The track then dropped down a 5 per cent, 1-mile grade to the junction with Southern's Murphy (N.C.) branch.

Despite its obvious attractions, the GC was a simple little line, and herein lies its appeal to the modeler. Hemmed in as it was by the mountains, it served only a few on-line industries and facilities. Its roster of equipment was small and its track arrangement simple.

History and operations

In 1905 a group of mountain men organized the Graham County Land & Transportation Company to move timber out of Graham County. Their plans also called for a through Atlanta-Knoxville (Tenn.) line which would have followed what later became GC right of way, but the GCL&TC never went beyond the planning stage. In 1916 a railroad was graded from Robbinsville to Topton by Whiting Manufacturing Company. Wooden bridges were built and some ties laid in place. A used 90-ton Baldwin rod-locomotive was purchased locally and sent to Asheville for overhaul. In July 1916 a flood swept through much of western Carolina and the Baldwin was washed away in the French Broad River never to be found again. With its one and only locomotive lost, the Graham County Railroad project came to a halt.

The early 1920's saw the Bemis Lumber Company moving south from Fishing Hawk, W. Va. — where the company already maintained their own standard-gauge Shay-operated railroad — to Robbinsville. Bemis Lumber Company completed the Graham County Railroad in 1925. Little No. 1 Shay from Bemis' West Virginia operations was used on GC construction trains. In February 1925 the GC's new 70-ton Shay arrived from Lima Locomotive Works. It sported the impressive number 1925 (for the year it was built, of course) and

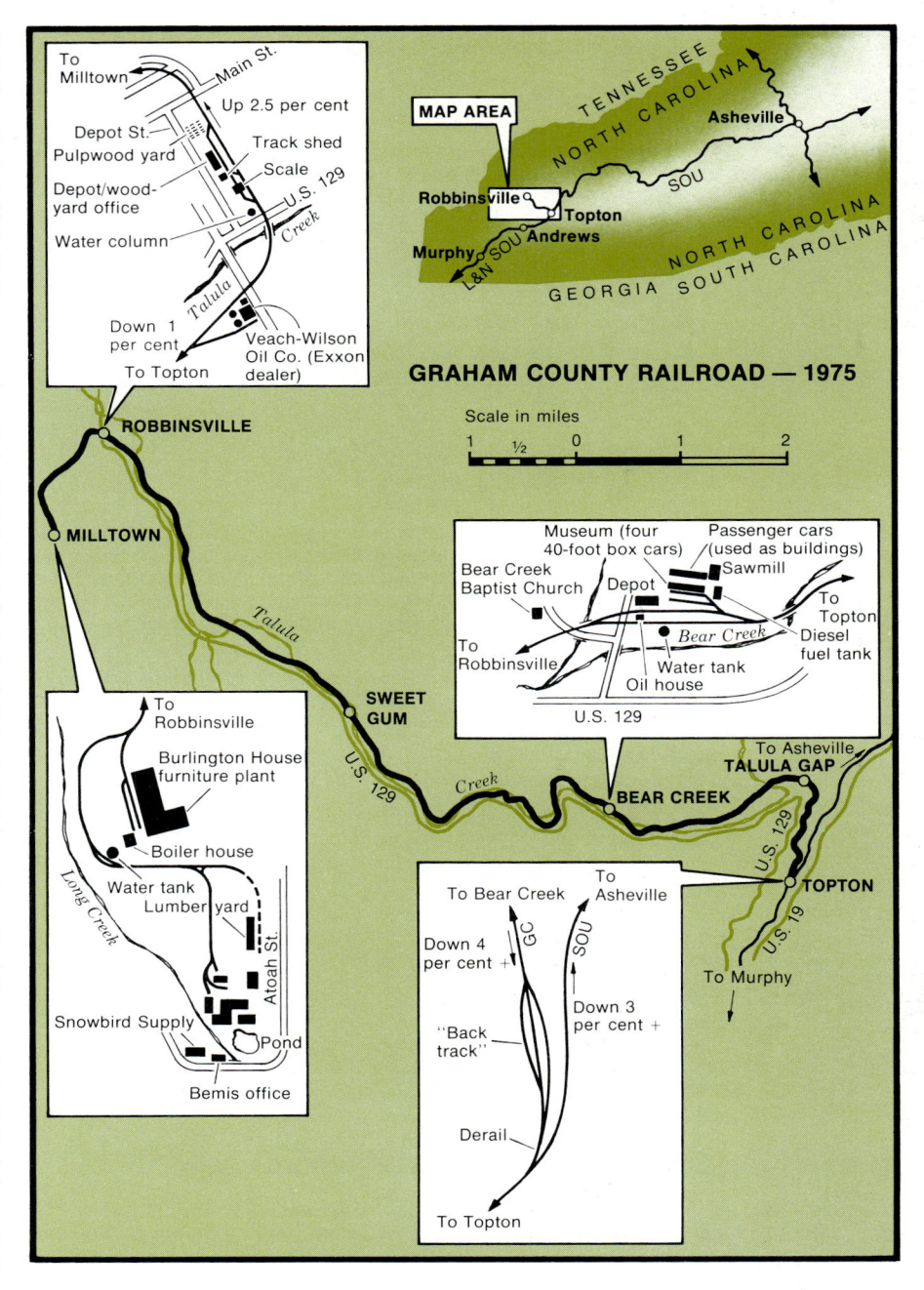

GRAHAM COUNTY RAILROAD — 1975

17

Mallory Hope Ferrell.

Geared locomotives tend to sound as if they're moving much faster than they really are, so judging by the smoke, the 1925 probably sounds as if it's doing 60 mph—although 6 mph would be more accurate. Note the frame gas station in the background.

Michael J. Dunn III.

Daniel F. Watson Jr.

(Top) GC used this ramp to coal its Shays. Hoppers were pushed to the top and their loads discharged into the bin below. Locomotives parked next to the bin to receive coal. (Above) Diesel 102 at Bear Creek.

William J. Husa Jr.

A latecomer, Shay 1923 subs for the 1925 (undergoing repairs) and the 1926 (condemned boiler) in October 1968. GC considered purchasing Canadian Shays to avoid estimated $12,000 repair tag on the 1926.

Hugh M. Jansen Jr.

After a runaway log car smacked her in the face, 1926's front was rebuilt; she inherited the number plate from Champion Fibre Shay 3229, scrapped in '42. This 1967 photo shows her at the coaling ramp.

Robert L. Hogan.

"Ole Sidewinder" name appeared on 1925's tank for a time, but management restored her more authentic GRAHAM COUNTY RAILROAD COMPANY lettering after this photo was taken in the early 1970's.

Frank Barry.

The 1926 labors northward out of Topton in July 1963. Foliage nearly engulfs the bluff-hugging right of way.

Robert L. Hogan.

Choice of numbers: The 1923 had a 112 number plate and a headlight/number panel from Northern Pacific 2-8-2 No. 1802.

Robert L. Hogan.

A model of the GC can include some rocky meadows (with grazing cows) bounded by slopes of hardwood trees.

The Robbinsville enginehouse was a corrugated metal structure with tall, double-sliding doors. A vented cupola on the roof allowed smoke to escape from inside the building. The enginehouse was located at the western extremity of the GC.

Two photos, Michael J. Dunn III.

Except for tourist runs out of the new Bear Creek station, the railroad never offered regular passenger service. GC's only original station was this freight-type depot at Robbinsville. The main line is to the left of the caboose.

was to be the only new locomotive ever to run on the line.

Following completion of the GC, Bemis Lumber Company began construction of a logging line called the Buffalo & Snowbird Railroad, which followed Atoah Creek west from its connection with the GC at Robbinsville. The B&S, in turn, connected at Junction, N. C., with a 3-foot-gauge logging railroad built by the Champion Fibre Company (but operated by Bemis).

Originally Shay 1925 doubled as a Graham County road engine and as a Bemis Lumber Company woods locomotive. During the day the Shay hauled log trains and at night made the run to the Southern connection near Topton.

In 1930 Bemis purchased the No. 4 Shay from the Hassinger Lumber Company of Konnarock, Va. The "Big 4" was an unusual four-truck job and was well liked by the crews, in spite of her cracked crank (veteran GC engineer Ed Collins stated that No. 4's main bearing used to get "pretty warm" at times). By 1936 or 1937 No. 4 was being used as a stationary boiler for a dry kiln and was scrapped around 1944.

In 1940 Bemis bought Shay 1926 from nearby Knox Power Company. The GC then loaned No. 1925 to the now-abandoned Tennessee & North Carolina Railroad, and the 1926 became the GC road engine. A minor skirmish with a runaway log car in the early 1960's necessitated the rebuilding of No. 1926's smokebox front and number plate using parts from one of the stored Champion Fibre narrow-gauge locomotives, Shay No. 3229. In the early 1960's the 1925 also was rebuilt.

Some interesting changes were implemented by the Graham County Railroad in the mid-1960's. By this time the GC Shays had become an informal tourist attraction, so the Graham County Railroad decided to use the popularity of its steam locomotives (as well as the spectacular Smokey Mountain scenery) to its advantage. The railroad teamed up with Bemis Hardwood Company, at that time still the GC's controlling interest at Robbinsville, and with the National Park Service and Government Services, Inc. to commence passenger service for the first time in GC's history. The alliance purchased a pair of Shays from Conasauga River Lumber Co. in Tennessee, the 112 and the 2147. No. 112, a 60-ton, two-truck Shay, was renumbered 1923 and went into service in August 1966; the 70-ton, three-truck 2147 went on display at Bear Creek, the chosen base for passenger operations. An authentic-looking period depot was constructed at Bear Creek, passenger cars were built at the GC shops in Robbinsville, and in June 1966 the "Bear Creek Junction Railroad" passenger operation of the Graham County Railroad was in business. A year later it was renamed the Bear Creek Scenic Railroad.

Passenger trains operated from Bear Creek station to Topton with a stop at the passing siding near the summit of the railroad, affording passengers a view of Nantahala Gorge from a specially built lookout platform. Passenger runs intermingled with freights; meets were scheduled at the summit passing track and at Bear Creek. In 1968 the 1925 was incapacitated by a mishap while in freight service, and the railroad suddenly found itself in a bind for locomotives — the 1926 already was out of service with a condemned boiler. So, No. 1923, nee 112, did double duty hauling freight and passengers while the 1925 was rebuilt using parts from the 1926.

In May 1970 the Bemis Lumber Company relinquished control of the GC; the Bear Creek Scenic operation lived on through the summer season of the year, after which all operations on the GC were concluded. It was feared that the GC had folded forever, but in July 1973 a company named Bear Creek Junction, Inc. revived Bear Creek Scenic Railroad passenger service and in September reopened the Graham County Railroad between Bear Creek and Topton. In January 1974 the GC was back in operation all the way to Robbinsville.

In that same month the GC acquired a former Savannah State Docks General Electric 70-ton diesel, GC No. 102, for its freight and mixed-train operations. Passenger service was provided by the 1925, but occasionally it saw freight service when a helper was needed or when 102 was being shopped. Also on the property in 1974 was Shay No. 36, an ex-Brimstone Railroad locomotive leased from the Southern. The 1923 had been sold in 1962 to the Oregon, Pacific & Eastern, and old 1926 continued to supply parts for the Shays still in operation.

The tonnage ratings for Shay 1925 and GE 102 were almost the same but the Shay normally could pull one more car because of its lower gear ratio and better adhesion.

From Robbinsville eastward over the summit to Topton the 1925 could handle from 425 to 450 tons, and the 102 could take about 400 to 425 tons. However, westward from Topton to Robbinsville, the 1925 could take only 200 to 225 tons as far as the summit, and the 102 could take only 180 to 200 tons up the grade to Tulula Gap.

As of 1975 GC and BC operations called for steam passenger service between Bear Creek and the rim of Nantahala Gorge (a 5-mile round trip), and diesel — and occasionally steam — mixed-train service round trip from Bear Creek to Topton (a 7-mile round trip) and from Bear Creek to Robbinsville (a 19-mile round trip).

On March 30-31, 1975, nature got the best of the GC when it dumped more than 7 inches of rain on the little railroad. Two bridges were washed out, requiring service to be cut back to Bear Creek. Two months later operations ended for good.

The GC from end to end

At the junction near Topton the only sign of civilization was the wedding of the two lines, where the rock-ballasted 85-pound rail of the Southern contrasted with the simple earth-ballasted 60-pound trackage of the GC. The GC

19

(Above left) The scale, scale track, and water pipe and platform were situated just east of Robbinsville station. (Above right) This chip loader stood at the Bemis mill in Robbinsville. Wood chips were carried to the top of the loader by conveyor belt. Wood-chip cars have high sides so they can carry a greater volume of the light material.

Two photos, Michael J. Dunn III.

had a small three-track yard near the junction switch. East of the switch the two companies' lines were carved on little hillside shelves, almost adjacent to each other and separated by a small rock-retaining wall. Southern's single-track line struggles upgrade from the east while the GC dropped downgrade, from the passing track at Tulula Gap, to the junction. The grade to Tulula Gap often meant that GC trains had to double between the junction yard and the passing siding (capacity, 10 cars) where cars were coupled into one train for the remainder of the trip to Bear Creek and Robbinsville. Following the line of least resistance, the track thereafter remained close to Tulula Creek, sometimes fording smaller creeks with culverts. It cut through farms and front yards before sneaking into the old station at Robbinsville.

Robbinsville, Graham County's seat, is a community of modest proportions. Because it is situated on a hilly rise, and because it was fairly well developed be-

fore the GC reached town in the mid-1920's, the railroad had to skirt the city on lower ground on a broad arc of track.

Near town was the station, a team track (used mostly for delivering building materials, merchandise, and farm supplies), dead-end scale track, and water pipe. The generous coaling stage a short distance upgrade from the station served triple duty: It supplied coal and sand for locomotives and coal for a local coal dealer before it was torn down in the early 1970's. By 1975 the Robbinsville depot was no longer used by the GC and served instead as an office for the Bristol Wood Yard.

Near the end of the arc of track was a large bulge where track was relocated several years ago around the two sides and back of a large tract of land in the narrowing valley. A large carpet factory (which later became the Burlington House furniture plant) was built here and a siding was put in for shipments to and from the plant.

Towards the western end of the GC's

line was the main reason for the GC's construction, the Bemis lumber properties. At one time a spur led to a lumber loading shed, where rough-cut planks and other lumber supplies were usually bundled and shipped on flat cars. The main track edged the drying yard and split three ways. One track led into the large corrugated-iron enginehouse and railroad shops adjacent to the mill. Parallel with the old enginehouse was a track on which live engines were kept between runs. Lying alongside and around this track was typical railroad litter: old cranes, retired cars, 1926's ruptured tank and dismantled tender, and an old Model A Ford on flanged wheels. To one side of the old shop a track reached a chute, where hoppers were loaded with wood chips. After a debarker stripped the sawlogs, the scraps left from sawing were shredded into chips and shipped out for use in paper manufacture.

The third track of importance — actually the last part of the main line —

(Above left) An air of prosperity seemed to surround the Robbinsville station area when this scene was photographed in December 1974 (compare with the 1961 depot scene on page 19). By this time the Bristol Wood Yard had acquired the depot, where we see pulpwood loading operations underway. **(Above right) A closeup of the pulpwood loader and pulpwood car.**

Two photos, Dan Ranger.

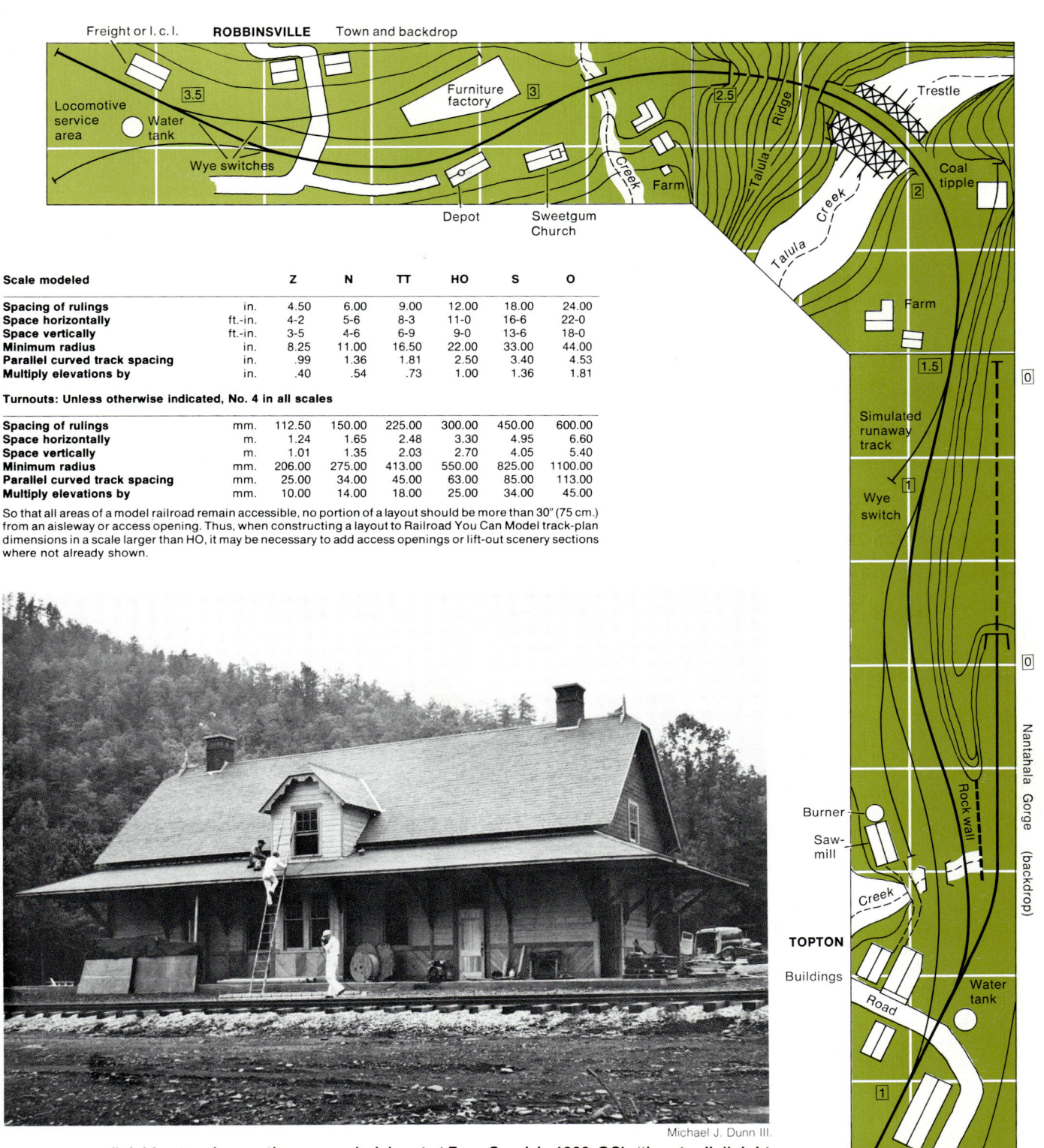

ROBBINSVILLE Town and backdrop
Freight or l.c.l.
Locomotive service area
Water tank
Wye switches
Furniture factory
Depot
Sweetgum Church
Farm
Talula Creek
Talula Ridge
Trestle
Coal tipple
Farm
Simulated runaway track
Wye switch
Burner
Saw-mill
Creek
TOPTON
Buildings
Road
Water tank
Station
Nantahala Gorge (backdrop)
Rock wall

Scale modeled		Z	N	TT	HO	S	O
Spacing of rulings	in.	4.50	6.00	9.00	12.00	18.00	24.00
Space horizontally	ft.-in.	4-2	5-6	8-3	11-0	16-6	22-0
Space vertically	ft.-in.	3-5	4-6	6-9	9-0	13-6	18-0
Minimum radius	in.	8.25	11.00	16.50	22.00	33.00	44.00
Parallel curved track spacing	in.	.99	1.36	1.81	2.50	3.40	4.53
Multiply elevations by	in.	.40	.54	.73	1.00	1.36	1.81

Turnouts: Unless otherwise indicated, No. 4 in all scales

Spacing of rulings	mm.	112.50	150.00	225.00	300.00	450.00	600.00
Space horizontally	m.	1.24	1.65	2.48	3.30	4.95	6.60
Space vertically	m.	1.01	1.35	2.03	2.70	4.05	5.40
Minimum radius	mm.	206.00	275.00	413.00	550.00	825.00	1100.00
Parallel curved track spacing	mm.	25.00	34.00	45.00	63.00	85.00	113.00
Multiply elevations by	mm.	10.00	14.00	18.00	25.00	34.00	45.00

So that all areas of a model railroad remain accessible, no portion of a layout should be more than 30" (75 cm.) from an aisleway or access opening. Thus, when constructing a layout to Railroad You Can Model track-plan dimensions in a scale larger than HO, it may be necessary to add access openings or lift-out scenery sections where not already shown.

Michael J. Dunn III.

Workmen put finishing touches on the new period depot at Bear Creek in 1966. GC's "leapty-dip" right of way was a liability for freight traffic, but an asset for passengers. Now travelers to Joyce Kilmer National Forest could take a thrilling ride into Nantahala Gorge behind authentic clanking Shays.

veered off from the shops and mill and crossed a little tree-lined creek in sight of a log pond. It then passed through the log-unloading yard of the sawmill. If the rail shipments of log were still in vogue (and the railroad still in business), the cars would be unloaded from a track beside the pond, but trucks later handled that service. The bungalow in front of the yard once housed the offices of the railroad and parent Bemis Lumber Company, but later housed only the offices for the Bemis Hardwood Lumber Company. Pulpwood loading was done nearby, where a dirt ramp had been improvised to facilitate transfer of pulpwood from truck to freight car. One track ended beside the warehouse portion of the Snowbird Supply Co. Beyond lay the hardwood glens of the Snowbird Mountains, once pierced by the logging trackage described earlier.

The track arrangement at what became the Bemis Hardwood Lumber Company was quite different by the mid-1970's. Only three tracks remained: the chip track (with a two-car capacity on a 42-degree curve), a lumber-loading spur (capacity, three cars), and the shop track.

Modeling notes

You say you haven't enough room for

GRAHAM COUNTY RAILROAD SIDINGS AND SPURS AS OF MAY 1929

Milepost	Station	Spur or siding name (if any)	Length (feet) Siding	Spur	Entrance*
0	Topton	One track	833		
0	Topton	Two track	833		
0	Topton	Back track	823		
0.3		Safety track		423	R
				317	R
1.3	Talula Gap	Gap siding	837		
1.7				227	T
3.3	Bear Creek	Bear Creek spur		453	R
4.5				358	R
4.5				194	T
5.4				250	R
5.8				277	R
6.2				352	T
7.8	Sweet Gum	Sweet Gum spur		457	R
10.4	Robbinsville	Veach-Wilson spur		991	T
11.0	Robbinsville	House track	650		
11.0	Robbinsville	Car house		238	T
11.0	Robbinsville	Coal dock		121	R
11.6	Robbinsville			140	R

*Trailing-point position:
T = Train headed toward Topton
R = Train headed toward Robbinsville
(If blank, siding can be entered from either end)

North Carolina brings to mind warm days and green vegetation, but this February 1964 vista of Nantahala Gorge reminds us that winter does find its way below the Mason-Dixon Line.

W. Frank Clodfelter.

a model railroad? Perhaps our compact shelf version of the Graham County Railroad can solve that problem. In HO scale, this layout will fit into a 9 x 12-foot room. Modeled in N scale, the layout will take up even less room (although N scale Shays are hard to come by, and you may have to settle for a dieselized Graham County). The railroad could be made semi-portable by dividing it into three modules that bolt together, ideal if you are an apartment dweller who moves from time to time.

We chose to represent the pre-passenger days of the Graham County Railroad, but the plan could be expanded to accommodate the later facilities at Bear Creek and include passenger service as well as freight.

Trackage in the real Robbinsville was quite spread out, but we have consolidated it into a few feet. The grade in the plan is a scale 6 per cent, but it can be made steeper for added effect. The idea is to make the grade steep enough to require a train to double over the hill, thus adding variety and interest to operations.

To make operation more interesting, we've added civilization to Topton. Bring a Southern Railway local freight out from the hidden holding track a couple of times a day to provide interchange traffic for the Graham County at Topton. The freight could consist of a black, off-white, and gold Geep, some freight cars, and a caboose.

Some freight cars? Yes, but not just any freight cars. The Graham County could not accept cars over 57 feet (over coupler knuckles) long, nor cars that grossed over 200,000 pounds. The following are the cars that were most commonly found on the GC in later years:

Box cars: Most box cars carried inbound loads for the Burlington furniture plant; most of them were Southern, although a few foreign roads showed up. The 40- and 50-foot single-door box cars were used for furniture, and the 50-foot double-door cars were used for dry kiln lumber.

Flat cars: Most flat cars that came in were Southern Railway 50-foot "chain flats," flat cars with stakes and chains, specially equipped to handle lumber.

Chip cars: These were actually Southern's 49-foot, six-bay "Big Red" coal hoppers specifically assigned to the Graham County to handle wood chips.

Wood racks: These were usually cars from the Southern, Central of Georgia, Savannah & Atlanta, or other SR-controlled lines, and all were stenciled "Load only to Canton, N. C." These cars have an 18- to 24-cord capacity (a cord of wood takes up approximately 128 cubic feet of space).

Gondolas: GC used short, low-side 40- or 52-foot gondolas from the Southern for timber and crossties.

We can make the layout even more operational by adding a freight-car forwarding system for these cars. Kalmbach's HOW TO OPERATE YOUR MODEL RAILROAD, by Bruce Chubb, describes some systems ideal for small layouts.

The track plan shown will work with No. 4 switches and flexible track, but with a small layout such as this, now might be the time to experiment with building your own switches and laying your own track. Scenicking should include numerous trees, some unpaved roads, and several weather-beaten frame buildings, including the Sweet-gum Church. But no matter how y'all build it, a model Graham County Railroad will provide hours of enjoyment and Southern hospitality.

H. Reid.

Engineer Ed Collins leans from the cab of 1925 to watch a time-honored tradition.

22

Boston-bound RDC 6122 will become a warm retreat for waiting passengers at Prides Crossing, Mass., on a wintry day in January 1975. The closings of station agencies have made depot properties available to other businesses, in this case a gift shop.

B&M's Gloucester branch

A B&M branch line in Massachusetts that's keyed to passenger operation

Steam era on the branch: Lucky photographer caught locals meeting near Manchester.

IN THE LATE 1840's the Eastern Railroad built a 17-mile branch northeastward from Beverly, Mass. (18 miles northeast of Boston) to Rockport. The principal source of traffic on the branch was the city Gloucester, noted then as now for its fishing industry. As the years passed, the Eastern became part of the Boston & Maine, and the towns along the Gloucester branch changed in character, first to seaside resorts and then to suburbs of Boston. The Gloucester branch is now part of the network of suburban lines operated by the Boston & Maine for the Massachusetts Bay Transportation Authority.

The Gloucester branch provides a fascinating railroad operation to model. The rolling stock used on the branch through the years was varied and interesting; the schedules called for frequent morning and evening commuter trains with midday local freight and passenger trains.

Operations on the branch

Let's follow a day of operation on the

23

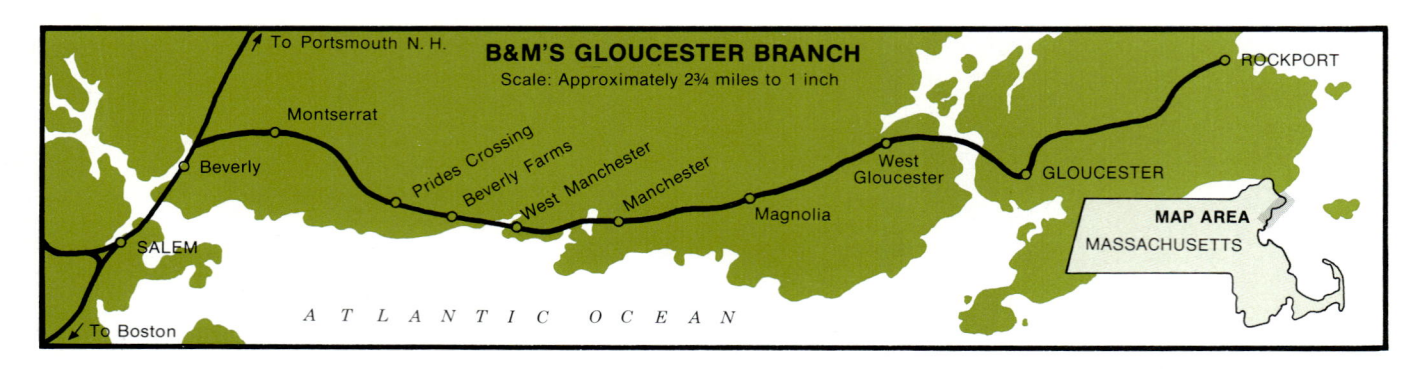

Blue, black, and white "McGinnis" livery (it appeared in the mid-1950's during the administration of B&M president Patrick McGinnis) could be found on Geeps on Rockport branch freights.

The 73-inch drivers of Class P-2-d Pacific 3656 (Alco, 1911) rolled many a commuter home to Rockport before the 4-6-2 was scrapped in 1956. B&M had more than 100 Pacifics.

branch in the early 1950's. The primary flow of traffic in the morning is toward Boston, so the line comes to life at its eastern end first. The first train leaves Rockport for Boston at 5:55 a.m., and the next leaves at 7 o'clock. At Gloucester the 7 o'clock train meets the first train from Boston, an all-stops local that carries a mail car. As soon as the mail train arrives at Rockport, the third train of the day rolls off to Boston, and just before 8 a.m. the *Cape Ann* heads out. The *Cape Ann*, one of three named commuter trains on the B&M, isn't a classic train; its distinction is that it makes no local stops after it reaches the Eastern Division main line at Beverly. The *Cape Ann* carries only coaches, but a parlor car added to the consist of your model *Cape Ann* would not be out of place — Boston's North Shore is no poverty pocket.

After the departure of the *Cape Ann*, activity settles into a regular pattern: Every hour or so a train arrives from Boston, backs around the reversing loop, and waits at the Rockport station until departure time. The midday local freight keeps out of the way of the passenger trains by ducking into industrial sidings and yard tracks.

Around 6 p.m. there is another flurry of activity as outbound rush-hour trains arrive Rockport and tie up for the night. A midevening train and a late evening train in both directions finish the day's activity. The midnight train from Boston carries the suburban editions of the morning papers.

The Sunday schedule lacks both the concentrations of trains during the rush hours and the local freight. In the late afternoon, though, the frequency of inbound trains is increased to carry city-dwellers back to Boston after an outing at the beaches.

During the 1920's and 1930's the Gloucester branch boasted a Pullman

Although these two scenes were not photographed on the Gloucester branch, they do show some of the interesting types of diesel power that could be found on any B&M local. (Above) EMD BL2 No. 1552 rushes Boston-bound train 3006 through Merrimack, N. H., in 1950. (Right) A maroon-and-yellow RS3 rolls Boston-Troy (N. Y.) train 57 through Concord, Mass.

sleeper that arrived from New York every Saturday morning and returned Sunday evening. The car was part of a New York-Portland (Me.) train that operated via Worcester, Lowell, and Salem, Mass., and Portsmouth, N. H. The Rockport car was set out at Salem and relayed to Rockport on the first morning train from Boston.

The industries along the Gloucester branch are mostly of the receiving type rather than the shipping type, as you would expect in the suburbs: lumber yard, fuel company, cement plant, wholesale grocer, and so on. New England's heavy industry is generally concentrated along the rivers (the rivers were a source of power) and not along the coast.

The branch was (and is) double track except for the last 3.7 miles from Gloucester to Rockport. Double-arm lower-quadrant semaphores, which were the standard B&M block signal in early years, have been replaced with searchlight signals. Track on the branch was laid with relatively light rail (code 70 would be appropriate for HO) and gravel ballast. Until the B&M fell upon lean years the track was well-maintained.

You might expect the scenery along the branch to be made up of fishing boats, lighthouses, and crashing surf. The view from the train, however, consists mostly of salt marshes, woodlands, and backyards. Only in a few places is the track within sight of salt water. Of course, modeler's license can move some of the trackage to a shoreline setting on your own layout, if you prefer.

The branch runs through a terminal glacial moraine, and the granite bones of the topography are close to the surface, especially between Gloucester and Rockport.

Equipment

During the steam days most of the passenger trains on the Gloucester branch were hauled by P-2-class Pacifics — small, plain-looking 73-inch-drivered machines. Occasionally a P-3 would appear on the branch. The P-3's were somewhat more powerful than the P-2's and sported Delta trailing trucks, drop-equalizer tender trucks, and red-and-white striping and italic letters. A 2-8-0 or an 0-6-0 usually handled the local freight.

Maroon-and-yellow diesels took over in the mid-1950's: GP7's, RS3's, and BL2's on the passenger trains and EMD switchers on the freight.

Before Budd RDC's (Rail Diesel Cars built by Budd Company of Philadelphia) took over all passenger service in the 1950's, single RDC's protected midday passenger runs, and conventional equipment was used on rush-hour trains.

Until the mid-1940's wooden open-platform coaches and combines were used on all the passenger trains, but the steel-coach era should furnish the most interesting modeling material. B&M purchased steel coaches secondhand from Reading, Pennsylvania, New York Central, Erie, and Lackawanna, bringing variety to the appearance of its trains (although that was not B&M's primary purpose).

Most stations along the Gloucester branch were hip-roofed wooden structures with long umbrella sheds along the platforms.

Modeling notes

The Gloucester branch is appealing to model because it is a finite and manageable chunk of railroad. The track plan models the branch from its terminal at Rockport almost to the junction with the Boston-Portsmouth main line at Bev-

(Above) A Rockport-bound RDC is about to scoot across the drawbridge on Manchester Harbor at Manchester-By-The-Sea in 1975. **(Below)** RDC's lay over at Rockport between runs, but station facilities are minimal: a parking lot, a platform, and a small shelter.

Both photos, Jack Towne.

Blue-and-white GP38-2 No. 203 is in charge of the twice-weekly way freight on this June day in 1974. Note the guardrails. 
Jack Towne.

You'll need industries like this cement plant at Gloucester to generate freight traffic on a model of the Rockport branch.
Jack Towne.

Train 2528 passes Magnolia depot in the 1940's when wood coaches were the rule.
Wayne Brumbaugh.

25

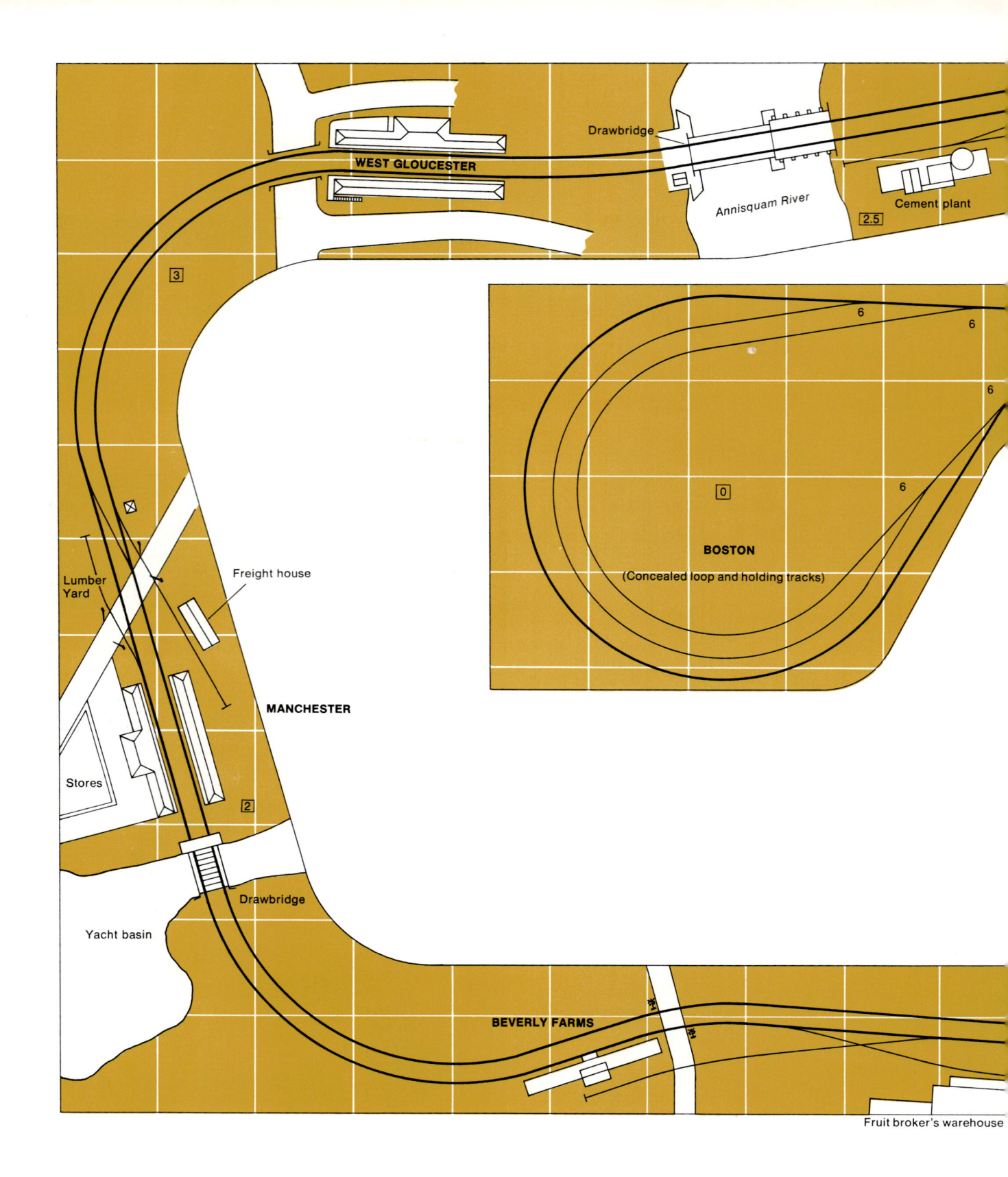

erly. Although not duplicated on our layout, the main line south of Beverly is also worthy of modeling, with attractions such as the yard, tunnel, and the old station at Salem.

The Salem station was demolished in the 1960's in a burst of modernism and civic uplift. It was a Norman fortress that straddled the tracks, defending the Salem tunnel — a short, low-clearance bore under the center of the city — from tall box cars. On your layout perhaps you could replace the plain wooden station at Gloucester with a more elaborate structure, such as a Norman fortress or a model of the Russian-Victorian B&M depot at North Conway, N. H.

The track plan is designed for an around-the-wall shelf layout, widened in one corner to accommodate the Rockport loop (a prototype for the "reverted loop" described by author John Armstrong in Kalmbach's TRACK PLANNING FOR REALISTIC OPERATION) and, hidden directly underneath it, the three-track "staging" loop that serves as the Boston end of the run.

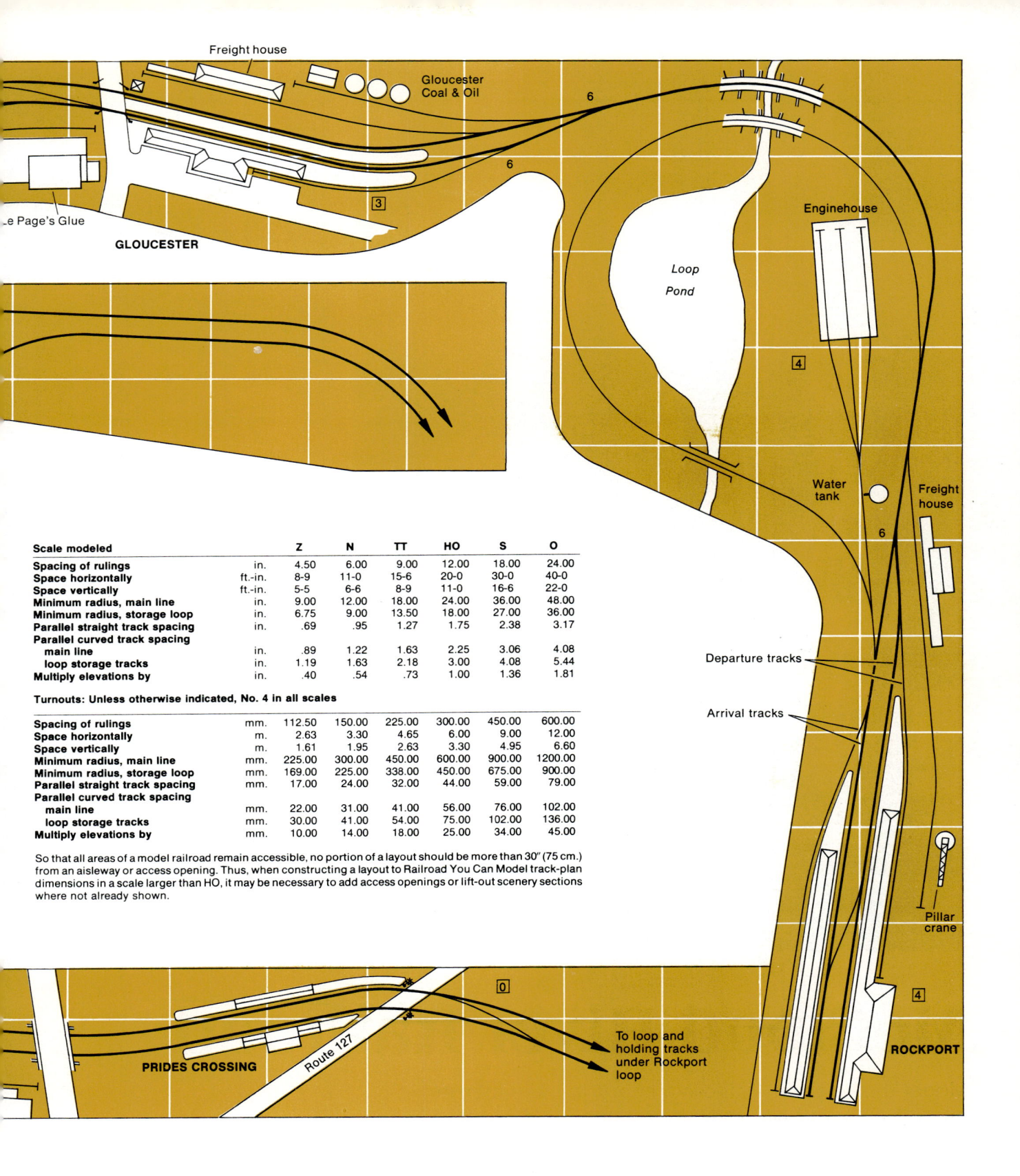

Scale modeled		Z	N	TT	HO	S	O
Spacing of rulings	in.	4.50	6.00	9.00	12.00	18.00	24.00
Space horizontally	ft.-in.	8-9	11-0	15-6	20-0	30-0	40-0
Space vertically	ft.-in.	5-5	6-6	8-9	11-0	16-6	22-0
Minimum radius, main line	in.	9.00	12.00	18.00	24.00	36.00	48.00
Minimum radius, storage loop	in.	6.75	9.00	13.50	18.00	27.00	36.00
Parallel straight track spacing	in.	.69	.95	1.27	1.75	2.38	3.17
Parallel curved track spacing							
main line	in.	.89	1.22	1.63	2.25	3.06	4.08
loop storage tracks	in.	1.19	1.63	2.18	3.00	4.08	5.44
Multiply elevations by	in.	.40	.54	.73	1.00	1.36	1.81

Turnouts: Unless otherwise indicated, No. 4 in all scales

Spacing of rulings	mm.	112.50	150.00	225.00	300.00	450.00	600.00
Space horizontally	m.	2.63	3.30	4.65	6.00	9.00	12.00
Space vertically	m.	1.61	1.95	2.63	3.30	4.95	6.60
Minimum radius, main line	mm.	225.00	300.00	450.00	600.00	900.00	1200.00
Minimum radius, storage loop	mm.	169.00	225.00	338.00	450.00	675.00	900.00
Parallel straight track spacing	mm.	17.00	24.00	32.00	44.00	59.00	79.00
Parallel curved track spacing							
main line	mm.	22.00	31.00	41.00	56.00	76.00	102.00
loop storage tracks	mm.	30.00	41.00	54.00	75.00	102.00	136.00
Multiply elevations by	mm.	10.00	14.00	18.00	25.00	34.00	45.00

So that all areas of a model railroad remain accessible, no portion of a layout should be more than 30" (75 cm.) from an aisleway or access opening. Thus, when constructing a layout to Railroad You Can Model track-plan dimensions in a scale larger than HO, it may be necessary to add access openings or lift-out scenery sections where not already shown.

We can closely simulate prototype branch operations. While passenger trains operate back and forth to Rockport according to a timetable — making passenger stops along the way, of course — the daily way freight could be making pickups and deliveries according to switchlists and waybills. (The way freight would be a special challenge because its work would have to be performed between the frequent passenger movements.)

The layout can provide operating pleasure for two or three people. Walk-around control would enable you to watch your models close-up as they roll through the scenery. The layout is small enough to allow you to devote more than usual attention to scenic details, and the simplicity of the track plan eases the task of wiring the layout. The pleasure produced by this type of layout will probably come in equal measure from operating trains over a stretch of track that resembles a real railroad and from watching your models at work in a logical setting.

(Left) Mount Shasta shimmers in icy splendor as a McCloud SD38 rolls the Burney local into Algomah, Calif., in February 1971. (Top) McCloud built this motor car to haul loggers. (Above) Two SD's on the "Mount Shasta Swing" returning from Pierce drop down the mountain on the McCloud leg of Signal Butte switchback in June 1971.

McCloud River Railroad

Model this popular California short line in either its past or present form, even if you can't fit a model Mt. Shasta into your layout room

MOST MODELERS automatically think of Shays, 30-pound rail, and rust when the subject of logging railroads comes up. In Northern California, though, logging railroad is synonymous with big diesels, extended-vision cabooses, all-door box cars, and lava-rock-ballasted track.

From Redding, Calif., north to Klamath Falls, Ore., 14,162-foot-high Mt. Shasta dominates the landscape, overshadowing the forests, canyons, and volcanic buttes. Just southeast of the snowcapped peak is the town of McCloud, Calif., headquarters of the McCloud River Railroad. The McCloud's rails head west from McCloud 16 miles to a connection with Southern Pacific at Mt. Shasta and east 65 miles to meet the Burlington Northern (formerly Great Northern) at Lookout, Calif. The last 34 miles, from Hambone to Lookout, are owned by BN but operated and maintained by the

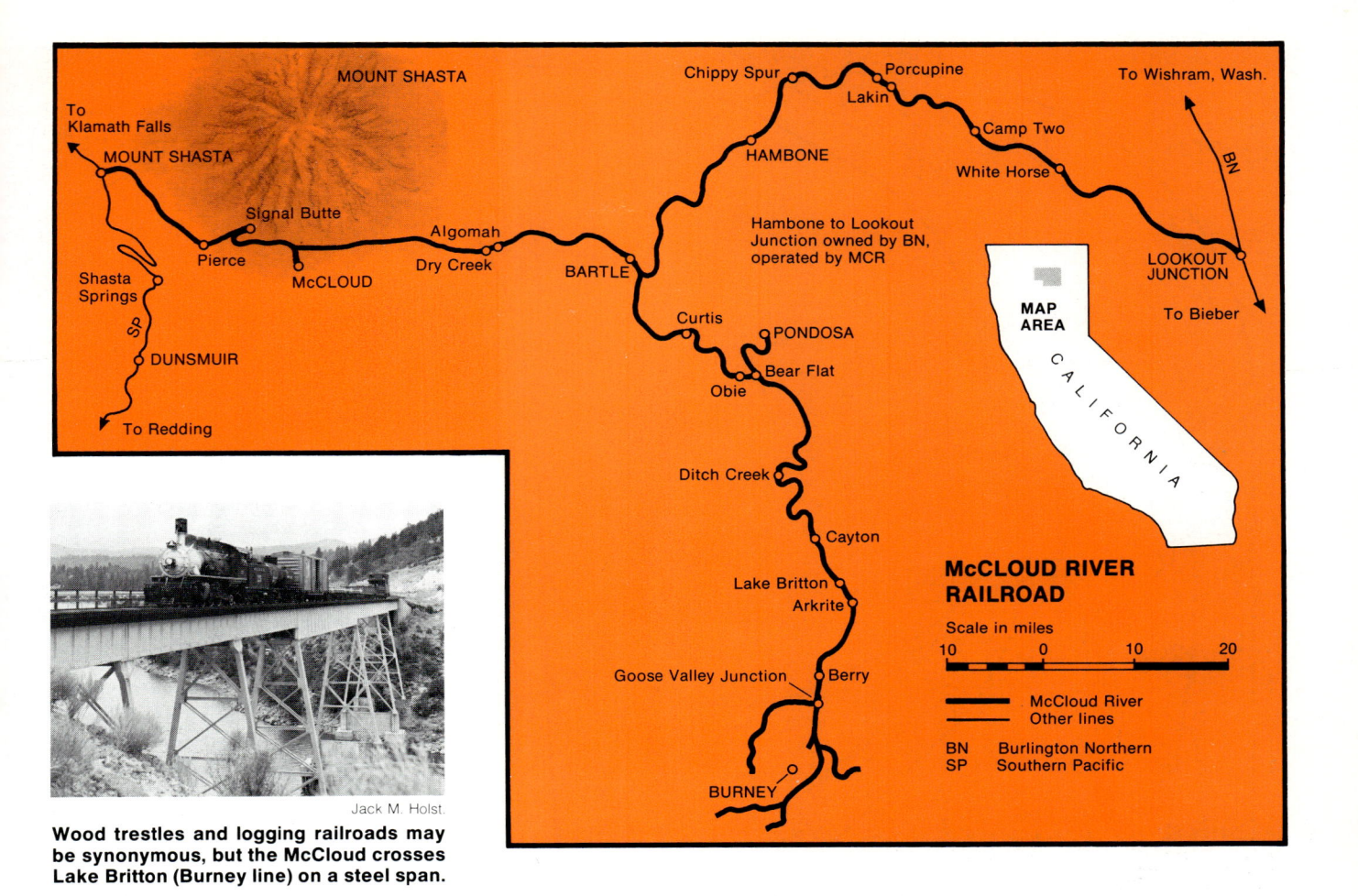

Wood trestles and logging railroads may be synonymous, but the McCloud crosses Lake Britton (Burney line) on a steel span.

McCloud's illustrious 2-6-2 No. 25 heels to Curve 43, a timber-hidden horseshoe curve near Obie, in a snow-dusted scene worthy of re-creation on a model McCloud. The train is en route to Pondosa with a January 1970 excursion.

Twin water tanks dominate this 1950's scene of a portion of Pondosa. The flat car with the homemade fencelike structure on it was used for carrying fuel wood. Pondosa was built in the middle 1920's as a model logging town.

McCloud. Western Pacific has trackage rights from Bieber, Calif., where it meets the BN, to Lookout and Hambone. McCloud's major source of carload freight is a line which drops south from Bartle, on the line to Hambone, to Burney.

History

The McCloud was chartered in 1897 to build from Upton, Calif., 3 miles north of Mt. Shasta on the SP, to Alturas, Calif., in the northeast corner of the state. The road also had its eye on Klamath Falls, just across the state line in Oregon. However, the McCloud's destiny was simpler. There was a lumber mill at Upton and there were trees on the slopes of Mt. Shasta. Within a few years the McCloud reached far enough into the woods that the lumber mill company decided to relocate in McCloud. In 1906 the railroad built a new line to connect with SP at Mt. Shasta (then called Sisson). The line to Upton was abandoned, as was indeed Upton itself. In 1907 the road began to extend its rails into the forests east of McCloud.

In the 1920's the Pacific Gas & Electric Company built several dams and powerhouses along the Pit River. The McCloud carried all the construction

29

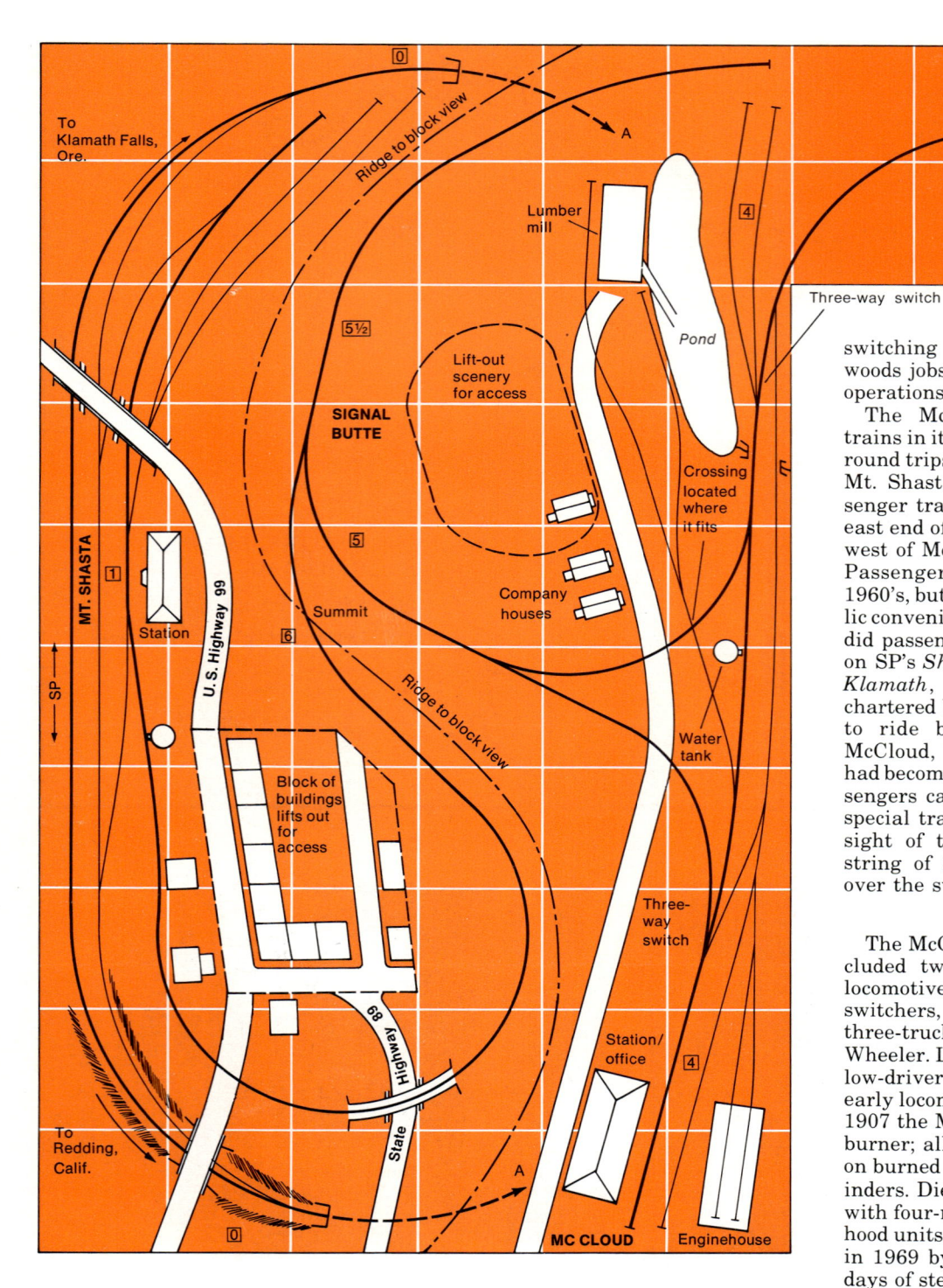

switching at McCloud and working woods jobs on the spurs to the logging operations.

The McCloud operated passenger trains in its earlier years — usually two round trips a day between McCloud and Mt. Shasta to connect with SP's passenger trains, plus a round trip to the east end of the line. After 1930, service west of McCloud was operated by bus. Passenger service resumed in the 1960's, but for a purpose other than public convenience and necessity. No longer did passengers for the McCloud arrive on SP's *Shasta Daylight*, *Cascade*, and *Klamath*, but instead they came in chartered busses and their own cars — to ride behind 2-6-2 No. 25. The McCloud, like many other short lines, had become a tourist carrier. Later, passengers came via SP and BN rails, in special trains. Fans could revel in the sight of the shining 2-6-2 pulling a string of SP stainless-steel Pullmans over the switchback on Mt. Shasta.

Equipment

The McCloud's early steam roster included two each of several types of locomotives — Moguls, six-wheel tank switchers, three-truck Heislers, and three-truck Shays — and a lone Ten-Wheeler. Later the line standardized on low-drivered Prairies and Mikados. The early locomotives were woodburners. In 1907 the McCloud received its first oil-burner; all its motive power from then on burned oil, in either fireboxes or cylinders. Dieselization was accomplished with four-motor and six-motor Baldwin hood units. The Baldwins were replaced in 1969 by three EMD SD38's. In the days of steam, the 2-8-2's usually were assigned to road hauls to Mt. Shasta and Lookout, and the 2-6-2's handled switching duties and woods jobs. In the Baldwin-diesel era, three units were needed for the daytime trip to Burney, and the nocturnal trips to the outside world called for two or three units. McCloud and Burney each required a unit for daytime switching duties. Current operations with only three units call for sharp motive-power dispatching and a high level of maintenance. Diesel-era steam assignments are uncomplicated. No. 25 can pull all of McCloud's passenger equipment easily. However, special trains, such as the 22-car special operated in February

materials in from the SP at Mt. Shasta to a junction with PG&E's own railroad, now long since abandoned, which distributed the materials to the construction sites.

In 1931 the Great Northern and the Western Pacific joined their lines at Bieber, forming the Inside Gateway route and breaking SP's monopoly in north-south transportation along the West Coast. The McCloud River built east to connect with a GN branch (and with WP through trackage rights) at Hambone. The railroad's most recent extension was in 1955 to Burney.

Throughout its history the McCloud, like other logging railroads, built spurs into the woods to follow lumbering operations and then later removed the tracks. Every few miles along the McCloud's right of way, trails of ties lead off into the forest (rails are expensive and can be reused; ties are cheap enough to leave in place when a spur is abandoned).

Nowadays one trip a day on each of McCloud's three lines provides sufficient service: a day run to Burney to take empties and bring back finished lumber, and night trips to the SP and BN interchanges. Only a few years ago, though, the McCloud's traffic included long trains of logs bound for the mill at McCloud. The rails were kept busy by

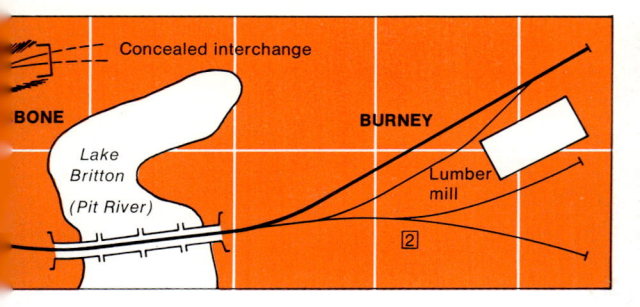

View from empty flats shows loaded cars. Logs were bundled with chains.

1969 by the Bay Area Electric Railroad Association, call for everything the McCloud has. That particular train required four Baldwins, No. 25 (to heat the cars and also for effect), a snowplow, and all the snow-shovelers that the road could muster — including its president.

Freight cars seen on the McCloud are wide-door box cars and wood-chip hopper cars of its two connections, a fleet of all-door box cars owned by McCloud's parent, U.S. Plywood, and, until a few years ago, hundreds of log flats. The wooden cabooses were of GN ancestry; today's cabooses are of the latest wide-cupola type. To judge by old photographs, the McCloud's passenger car fleet was made up of three open-platform wooden cars — a combine and a coach-observation, both elegant and arch-windowed, and a second combine, much more utilitarian — and a homemade motor car that looked like a dropout from McKeen-car school. The excursion-era roster comprises two ex-SP Harriman-style 60-foot coaches and two flat cars with benches and railings. They are painted bright red, as are the caboose and the SD38's.

Geography on the McCloud

If the McCloud were suddenly transported to the prairies of Illinois it would still be an interesting short line. Northern California's geography, though, makes the road especially fascinating. East of McCloud the line runs through the forest, generally crosswise to the creeks and rivers in the area. The line is neither level nor straight. The line to Burney crosses Lake Britton on a high steel trestle. West of McCloud — this is what we've been saving for you modelers — the line climbs over a shoulder of Mt. Shasta. There are stretches of 4.4 per cent grade and a genuine switchback, at Signal Butte, 5 miles west of and 1000 feet above McCloud. The grade and the 27-car length of the tail track limit the length of the freights on the west end of the railroad. Trains operate frontwards between Mt. Shasta and Signal Butte and backwards between McCloud and the switchback.

Modeling notes

What makes the McCloud a good railroad to model? Before the diesel it was as classic a logging railroad as you could want. When the silver-and-red Baldwins arrived, the railroad simply changed motive power, not the mode of operation. Later, when the McCloud ceased hauling logs and carried only finished products, there was compensation in the form of No. 25 and the excursion trains. If you model the McCloud of the late 1960's, you can have many contrasts — log flats and wide-door box cars, diesels and steam, passengers and

Scale modeled		Z	N	TT	HO	S	O
Spacing of rulings	in.	4.50	6.00	9.00	12.00	18.00	24.00
Space horizontally	ft.-in.	5-5	7-3	10-11	14-6	21-9	29-0
Space vertically	ft.-in.	3-9	5-0	7-6	10-0	15-0	20-0
Minimum radius, SP main	in.	11.25	15.00	22.50	30.00	45.00	60.00
Minimum radius, MCRR	in.	6.75	9.00	13.50	18.00	27.00	36.00
Parallel straight track spacing	in.	.71	.98	1.31	1.80	2.45	3.26
Multiply elevations by	in.	.40	.54	.73	1.00	1.36	1.81
Turnouts: unless otherwise indicated, No. 4 in all scales							
Spacing of rulings	mm.	112.50	150.00	225.00	300.00	450.00	600.00
Space horizontally	m.	1.63	2.18	3.26	4.35	6.53	8.70
Space vertically	m.	1.13	1.50	2.25	3.00	4.50	6.00
Minimum radius, SP main	mm.	281.00	375.00	563.00	750.00	1125.00	1500.00
Minimum radius, MCRR	mm.	169.00	225.00	338.00	450.00	675.00	900.00
Parallel straight track spacing	mm.	18.00	24.00	33.00	45.00	61.00	82.00
Multiply elevations by	mm.	10.00	14.00	18.00	25.00	34.00	45.00

So that all areas of a model railroad remain accessible, no portion of a layout should be more than 30" (75 cm.) from an aisleway or access opening. Thus, when constructing a layout to Railroad You Can Model track-plan dimensions in a scale larger than HO, it may be necessary to add access openings or lift-out scenery sections where not already shown.

Dieselization began on the McCloud in 1948 with the arrival of No. 28 (below left), a 1500-h.p. Baldwin DRS-6-6-15. Sister unit 29 arrived in 1950. The 28 was built with reduced weight to cope with 50-pound rail still being used on McCloud property. Dieselization was completed in 1954, and entirely with Baldwin products. RS-12's 32 (above left) and 33 were delivered in 1955, perhaps in anticipation of additional business created by the new Burney line. (Above right) No. 34, an AS-616, had 1000 more h.p. than the similar DRS units 28 and 29. (Below right) S-8 No. 31 arrived in 1953.

Four photos, Don Hansen.

31

(Above left) Lanky Mikado 26 steams at Bartle in May 1941. McCloud bought the 2-8-2, built by Alco in 1915, from the Copper River & Northwestern in Alaska. (Above right) No. 20 was a classy little Baldwin 2-6-2 built in 1924. (Below left) Perhaps the luckiest locomotive of McCloud's steam fleet was Alco-built No. 25, a compact 2-6-2 that managed to avoid the scrap dealer. She was pulled from service in the mid-1950's, but she steamed out of storage in 1963 (and worked on into the 1970's) and again shared trackage with the diesels that supplanted her brethren. (Below right) No. 19 was a 2-8-2 that served on two Arkansas properties before coming to the McCloud — by way of Mexico where it served with United Mining & Smelting.

freight. The McCloud isn't as exotic as the classic logging railroad, but there is enough left from McCloud's early days to contrast with the modernity of its equipment.

Our track plan condenses the west end of the railroad into a 6 x 10-foot layout in HO scale. Southern Pacific's main line is represented by an oval of track with a visible passing siding at Mt. Shasta and a concealed holding track underneath McCloud. A pair of freight trains, one in each direction, can appear from time to time to pick up and set out cars on the interchange tracks. The holding tracks can also conceal an SP *Cascade* (Alco PA's on the point, of course) or an Amtrak *Coast Starlight*, to furnish a contrast to McCloud's excursion train.

Let's take a ride on our model McCloud River Railroad. Since Amtrak does not stop at Mt. Shasta, nor did SP in later years, we've come into town by bus and hiked over to the station. A short freight is waiting. As we climb up into the cab an SP freight rolls past heading for Roseville, near Sacramento. The whine of the dynamic brakes of its three SD45's, big sisters of our SD38, momentarily drown out the chant of our engine. Behind our red-and-white diesel are three wide-door box cars, two wood-chip hoppers, and a caboose. The freight cars are empty, so our train length is limited more by the length of the tail track at Signal Butte than it is by the grade. Nevertheless, the 4 per cent grade is a challenge to 2000 h.p., 16 cylinders, and six traction motors.

The engineer releases the brakes and notches out the throttle, and we begin to move. The yard is relatively level, but the climb begins right at the turnout in front of the depot. We roll past the back doors of the gas stations, cafes, and motels that flank U. S. 99 and then swing left across the highway, protected by crossing flashers. The grade and the curve continue as we make a horseshoe around the town and cross state route 89, the highway to McCloud, on a short timber trestle. The trees soon block out all but occasional glimpses of the town below. We have spectacular views south down the Sacramento River canyon and north to Black Butte, a huge cone of volcanic cinders a few miles north of town. It stands like a sentinel over the junction of SP's Siskiyou and Cascade

Locomotives, snowplows, and other equipment are stored in this two-track shed at McCloud. The building would make a relatively easy modeling project.

Another structure with straightforward architecture and easy modeling possibilities: the steel office building/diesel shop that replaced McCloud roundhouse.

32

(Above left) Twins 22 and 23 double-head a log train near Pondosa in 1947. Both 2-6-2's were built by Alco in 1925; they had the same dimensions, weight, and tractive effort. (Above right) The 19 awaits assignment at McCloud in 1948.

lines. The Siskiyou line is the old route north to Portland via Ashland and Grants Pass; the Cascade line via Klamath Falls rejoins the original line at Eugene.

From the summit the line is (naturally) downhill, but the job of our crew is no easier. The 15-mph speed limit between McCloud and Mt. Shasta doesn't mean much to uphill trains; downhill it requires co-ordination of the dynamic and air brakes to keep under the limit. The task is harder eastbound, because trains back down into McCloud.

The turnout at the switchback is lined for us, so we roll onto the tail track past an abandoned turntable. There is so little level ground that the turntable pit rail and the walkway (it was an Armstrong's Patent-type turntable) had to be supported by trestlework. The rear brakeman throws the switch, and we start down into McCloud, caboose first.

As we curve onto the north leg of the wye past a row of nearly identical houses (McCloud for many years was a company town), the engineer gives several blasts of the horn — a whistle signal not found in the rule book. It tells the train crew's families that it's time to get dinner on the table. We spot the empty freight cars on the spur between the lumber mill and the line to Hambone, set the caboose in front of the rustic-looking station (it looks more like a mountain lodge than a railroad structure), and put the diesel on the lead to the square corrugated-steel enginehouse.

The model McCloud should be a study in contrasts. The SP track should have heavy rail, rock ballast, broad superelevated curves, and signals. The McCloud track should have light rail (code 70 for HO — the prototype is mostly 85- and 90-pound rail) and sharp curves. No weeds, though, and keep those ties straight: McCloud keeps its track in good shape. The rust-red lava-rock ballast of the McCloud is a distinctive note. Full-length passenger cars can be operated around the curves of our model McCloud if you do some modification of the running gear. They will look out of place, which is true to prototype.

The scenery on the two sides of the layout should differ. To make McCloud look as tranquil and woodsy as possible, Mt. Shasta should exemplify the worst in commercial strip zoning: gas stations, motels, cafes, drive-ins, and so forth. The prototype is a far more pleasant-looking town than we've depicted, but your aim in the model is to make McCloud look as far off the beaten track as possible. Thus you *need* a Shastavista Motel, a Wagon Wheel cafe, a Ponderosa restaurant, and an El Dorado Motor Court. (The names are interchangeable; every town west of Denver has an El Dorado something.) A high ridge or a double faced backdrop in the center of the layout will keep the two scenes visually separated. Vegetation, as you would expect, runs heavy toward trees, but there are areas, especially at the eastern end of the line, that have been cut over in recent years and are now grassland or scrub.

If you have space, by all means extend the line "east" from McCloud on a shelf. You can simulate the BN-WP interchange at Lookout with a concealed storage track, and the steel trestle across Lake Britton would be an interesting change from the timber trestle found on nearly everyone else's layout.

If you have space to expand the main part of the layout, add more twists and turns to the line rather than simply increasing the radius of the curves. Feel free to model an abandoned spur or two — or a working spur or two if you model the McCloud's log-carrying years.

So there you have it: a logging railroad that's different from the others, with enough variety in operation to keep you satisfied for a long time.

McCloud's two RS-12's and S-8 No. 31 triple-head out of Burney in 1964. The final paint scheme that appeared on the Baldwins was silver with red stripes, black lettering.

33

Horseshoe history: A trio of Brunswick green F units growls toward the summit of the Alleghenies with a St. Louis hotshot in the Indian summer of 1955. Meanwhile, a 2-10-4 is regaining its stride after an unexplained pause at the apex of the curve.

Old sign at the entranceway to the park at Horseshoe offered vital statistics to visitors. It has since been replaced.

Thunder on Horseshoe, June 1, 1953: J1-class 2-10-4 No. 6408 is determined to move that tonnage over the summit.

PRR's Horseshoe Curve and Gallitzin tunnels

Whether you model an era of Pennsy Class M1 4-8-2's or Amtrak SDP40F's, Horseshoe Curve is a fine setting for heavy-duty mountain railroading

WITNESS WITH US, if you will, one of the most breathtaking sights in American railroading today: We're aboard Amtrak's westbound *Broadway Limited*, about to depart Altoona, Pa., and begin the climb through the evening darkness to the summit of the Allegheny Mountains over world-famous Horseshoe Curve. Two blasts of the horn signal our departure; in minutes the lights of Altoona are behind us and our train is grinding upgrade in the night-shrouded mountains.

Soon we charge beneath a signal bridge — the amber beams of the position-light signals glinting off the stainless-steel car sides — and cant into sweeping Horseshoe Curve. Magnificent indeed is the sight of our 18-car streamliner, bound from New York and Washington to Chicago, stretched out around Horseshoe. As we approach the halfway point of the curve the moonlight reveals the Pennsylvania Railroad K4-class 4-6-2 on display in Horseshoe Curve park standing vigil in the shadows of mountains she once conquered. All too soon, this grand nighttime vista of Horseshoe fades as our train swings south toward the valley of Sugar Run.

Horseshoe Curve stands as a tribute to the once-great Pennsylvania Railroad and its builders, who foresaw that the PRR main line through the Alleghenies would be an important link between East and West. Penn Central Transportation Company, born of merger between the New York Central and Pennsylvania railroads in 1968, then held title to this great feat of engineering wedged in the Alleghenies

Cresson has been shortened (of course, if you have the space you may want to move Cresson farther from Gallitzin), and beyond Cresson the trains disappear into a tunnel and circle down to Altoona over a hidden loop.

If necessary, the tracks inside the tunnel between Cresson and Antis (this particular tunnel has no prototype) can be used as holding tracks. Through proper use of the crossovers at Gallitzin and Cresson, trains can be routed around those that are holding on the mainline tracks in this tunnel. Remember that all hidden trackage on the layout must be readily accessible in the event of a derailment or other problems that have a bad habit of occurring in tunnels.

Generally, eastbound trains use tracks 1 and 2, and westbound trains use 3 and 4. Freights that do not need to be switched but yet require helpers stop on track 4 — short of the passenger station if feasible (so as not to block "passengers" that may be "walking" between the station waiting room and passenger trains standing on track 2 or 3). The helpers move out of the yard on the east lead and cross over to 4 to couple to westbound freights. Westbound freights that have switching requirements must cross over at Antis to enter the yard. Most maneuvers for entering Altoona can be accomplished at Slope or Antis; other crossovers on the layout are used primarily by faster trains overtaking slower ones.

Scenicking Horseshoe Curve will be a challenge, but a rewarding one if the modeler observes a few basic rules of nature and geography. You might consider modeling Horseshoe in an autumn setting. Pennsylvania autumns are ablaze with color and the results would be breathtaking. Because of space limitations, we can't go into detail about scenery building here, but you will find Kalmbach's SCENERY FOR MODEL RAILROADS (and perhaps some earth science books from your local library) indispensable. Also, study the photographs and the layout plan that accompany this article and note where peaks, valleys, outcroppings, cuts, and fills are located in relation to one another and to the railroad right of way.

The highest point of your mountain terrain, of course, should be the summit of the Alleghenies, represented by the dotted line on the layout plan. The summit on the layout separates Gallitzin and Cresson from Horseshoe and Altoona. You should not be able to see Gallitzin and Cresson from Horseshoe and Altoona and vice versa. Remember when modeling Gallitzin that the town does not lie in a flat area — its houses, stores, and streets are perched on hillsides throughout the town, like a miniature San Francisco. Because Altoona lies in a wide valley, most of the down-

(Top) Six-axle Baldwin sharknose passenger units — unique to the PRR — coast through April snows in 1948 at Gallitzin. Note how the left side of the signal bridge is supported by the bank of the cut. **(Middle)** Eastbound J1 6436 heads through Allegrippus Gorge, where the right of way lies not far below the mountaintops. Bennington curve is beyond the signal bridge. **(Bottom)** An ex-PC GP35 and a Conrail U25B and GP40 provide early morning westbound action near Cresson in November 1976.

43

(Above) A 1974 view of the main (highway) level of Horseshoe Curve park shows the display caboose, gift shop, and refreshment stand. The tunnels beyond the cars carry Burgoon Run and the highway beneath the tracks. **(Right)** Track level is dozens of steps up from the main level. This part of the park remains virtually unchanged from this 1950's scene — except for those Baldwin Centipede helpers dropping downhill.

town area (which has some fairly large buildings) is flat. Altoona yard (we have taken modeler's license to move it to the south side of the main line) can be expanded or trimmed from what the plan shows, depending on the amount of room you have and how much interest you have in switching and yard work.

Let's go through a couple of theoretical train movements using the layout plan. A westbound Pennsy TrucTrain behind three SD45's rolls into Altoona and stops on track 4 to pick up a set of helpers, two RSD15's. Once the helpers are attached, the piggybacker departs. At the same time, a passenger train (let's say it's the Pittsburgh-bound *Dusquesne* behind a brace of tuscanred E's) departs Altoona on track 3. Chances are the passenger will have overtaken the TrucTrain before Horseshoe. If the TrucTrain's helpers will be needed back at Altoona right away they can be uncoupled at UN tower and sent around the wye to go back east, or they can be removed at Cresson (to wait, perhaps, for an eastbound train needing dynamic braking assistance). If helpers are to be uncoupled at UN, the TrucTrain will have to be crossed over to track 3 at MG. But suppose the passenger train leaves Altoona several minutes behind the TrucTrain. There's a chance that the TrucTrain will block the passenger at Cresson while dropping off helpers. The TrucTrain could

Problems for the dispatcher, May 14, 1967: A derailment east of Allegheny Tunnel has brought a train of westbound empties on track 3 to a halt at Horseshoe (left to right, track 4, 3, 2, 1). Meanwhile, a TrucTrain on 4 — the only open westbound track — is about to overtake the helpers of the stalled freight while an eastbound eases downhill on track 1. Once the TrucTrain is clear, the empty train will probably cross to track 4 at MG tower.

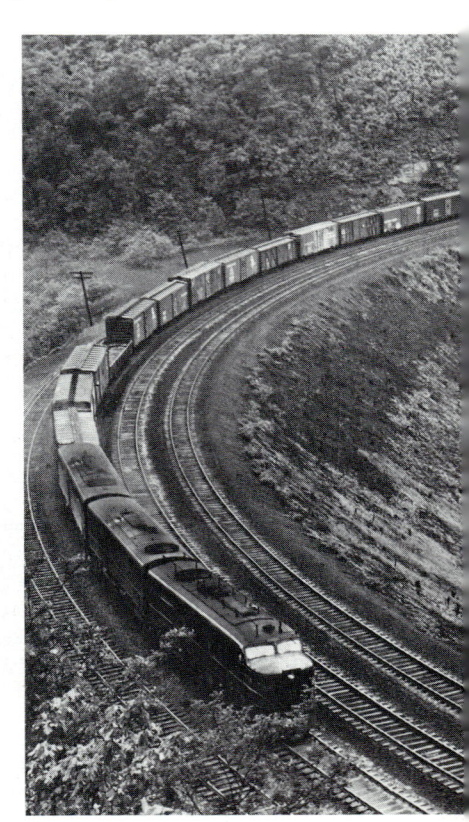

44

This rare, early view of Kittanning Point station, the Altoona reservoirs, and the two calks of Horseshoe Curve (the curve itself is to the back of the photographer) shows the higher elevation — about 122 feet — of the south calk, where an eastbound train (circled) has just appeared. The stone depot was torn down many years ago, probably soon after Pennsy discontinued the Kittanning Point station stop during the 1930's.

hold at MG to let the passenger around it, but stopping a freight train moving upgrade could cause problems. It might be wiser to "wrong main" the passenger at MG, run it through Gallitzin on track 2 via AR, and cross it back over to track 3 at Antis if eastbound traffic is light.

To make operation a little more interesting (and challenging for the dispatcher) we've included some industrial spurs at Altoona, Gallitzin, and Cresson. Certain mainline freights should stop at Altoona yard to drop off blocks of cars destined to these spurs or the branchline interchange at Cresson. A local freight can then deliver the cars to their proper destinations, perhaps using one of the freight-car forwarding systems discussed in Kalmbach's HOW TO OPERATE YOUR MODEL RAILROAD, by Bruce Chubb. (Mainline trains should not stop at Gallitzin or Cresson to switch, even though they may have cars destined to these towns.)

Our model Cresson has limited storage capacity for helpers, so don't let things get clogged there. Of course, when you add still more trains to the operation, train movements could get very interesting. Invite fellow modelers over some evening, give one of them the dispatcher's job (and plenty of pity), assign each of the remaining fellows a train, and you are in for a night of heavy mainline railroading, Horseshoe Curve style!

(Left) A-B-B Alco FA's churn up track 3 at almost the exact location of the "dispatcher's problems" scene on the facing page, but 14 years prior. (Above) A panoramic view of the curve taken in the 1950's clearly shows Kittanning Point, the park (note the giant horseshoe near the flagpole), and part of the Altoona reservoirs. The eastbound train traveling on what normally are the westbound tracks is probably the Gotham Limited from Chicago.

45

TRAINS: Wallace W. Abbey.

KALMBACH BOOKS: Mike Schafer.

(Left) Two Milwaukee traditions: Fairbanks-Morse switchers and breweries. The MILW H12-44 is pulling cars over a scale track. **(Above)** The Beer Line provides an ideal prototype for industrial switching.

Milwaukee Road's Beer Line

The branch line that helped make Milwaukee famous

KALMBACH BOOKS: Mike Schafer.

The Beer Line starts at Glendale Yard, North Milwaukee, about 4 miles from downtown. In this 1977 view looking south, Glendale Yard is in the background; the stucco depot sits at the junction of MILW's Milwaukee-Green Bay line (foreground) and its North Milwaukee-Portage (Wis.) secondary line. The Beer Line branches to the left, and North Milwaukee tower (left of the yard) sits in the wye formed by the Beer Line junction.

THE MILWAUKEE ROAD'S busiest branch is a 6-mile line that serves the northeast segments of downtown Milwaukee, Wis. Officially it's the Chestnut Street line, but most people call it the Beer Line. The biggest industry on the branch is the Joseph Schlitz brewery. The Pabst brewery, another major customer, is located on a hill a few blocks west of the track. The Beer Line isn't exclusively a beer carrier; many industries besides the one that made Milwaukee famous are located on the branch.

History

The line was built in 1854 as part of the La Crosse & Milwaukee Railroad. It extended north from Chestnut Street (now Juneau Avenue) along the west bank of the Milwaukee River and then turned northwest through North Milwaukee, the junction with what is now the Milwaukee Road's line to Green Bay.

Chestnut Street at one time was the terminal for passenger trains to the north. As time passed and various railroads were consolidated to form the

46

TRAINS: Wallace W. Abbey.

An H12-44 in an early MILW paint scheme of gray and orange pulls a 40-car transfer train northward from Glendale Yard onto the south wye track leading to the Beer Line. Photo was snapped from the tower.

KALMBACH BOOKS: Mike Schafer.

A view to the southwest from Holton Street reveals many modeling possibilities— switchbacks, multilevel tracks, and street-running to name a few. The Beer Line main and the yard leads to Humboldt Yard (behind the photographer) are at right. Empty cars destined for the bottling plant are held in the small yard near the center of the photo. Elevators A and B (white building) dominate the Schlitz brewery complex.

Milwaukee Road, the city of Milwaukee also grew. The heart of downtown Milwaukee wound up right between the end of the Chestnut Street line and the Milwaukee Road's principal passenger station. Extending the Chestnut Street line south to connect with the Chicago-Milwaukee main line at the station was impossible, not because of the distance — seven blocks — but because of the expense of the land. So, Chestnut Street passenger trains were routed to the main station around two sides of a triangle, and the almost-hypotenuse stretch of track — the Chestnut Street line — became freight only.

Modeling

The Beer Line is almost a one-commodity railroad. For years experts have advocated modeling many small and diverse industries on a layout rather than one large industry. However, one well-chosen large industry can allow the same variety of cars and the same complexity of switching moves in less space than a multiplicity of small industries. Using the brewery as an example, a grain elevator and a bottling plant can logically be much closer together than, say, a wholesale grocer and a bulk-oil storage facility.

By cutting, bending, and condensing we can fit the last mile or so of the Beer Line onto a 4 x 8-foot sheet of plywood. The lower level of the layout includes a small yard and a second track around half the oval. The latter requires a curved turnout; if you can't obtain a curved turnout, substitute an ordinary one and sacrifice a couple of car-lengths of space.

From the yard a track climbs to the upper level, which could be constructed on a second sheet of plywood double-decked over the concealed part of the lower level.

The buildings of the brewery are the

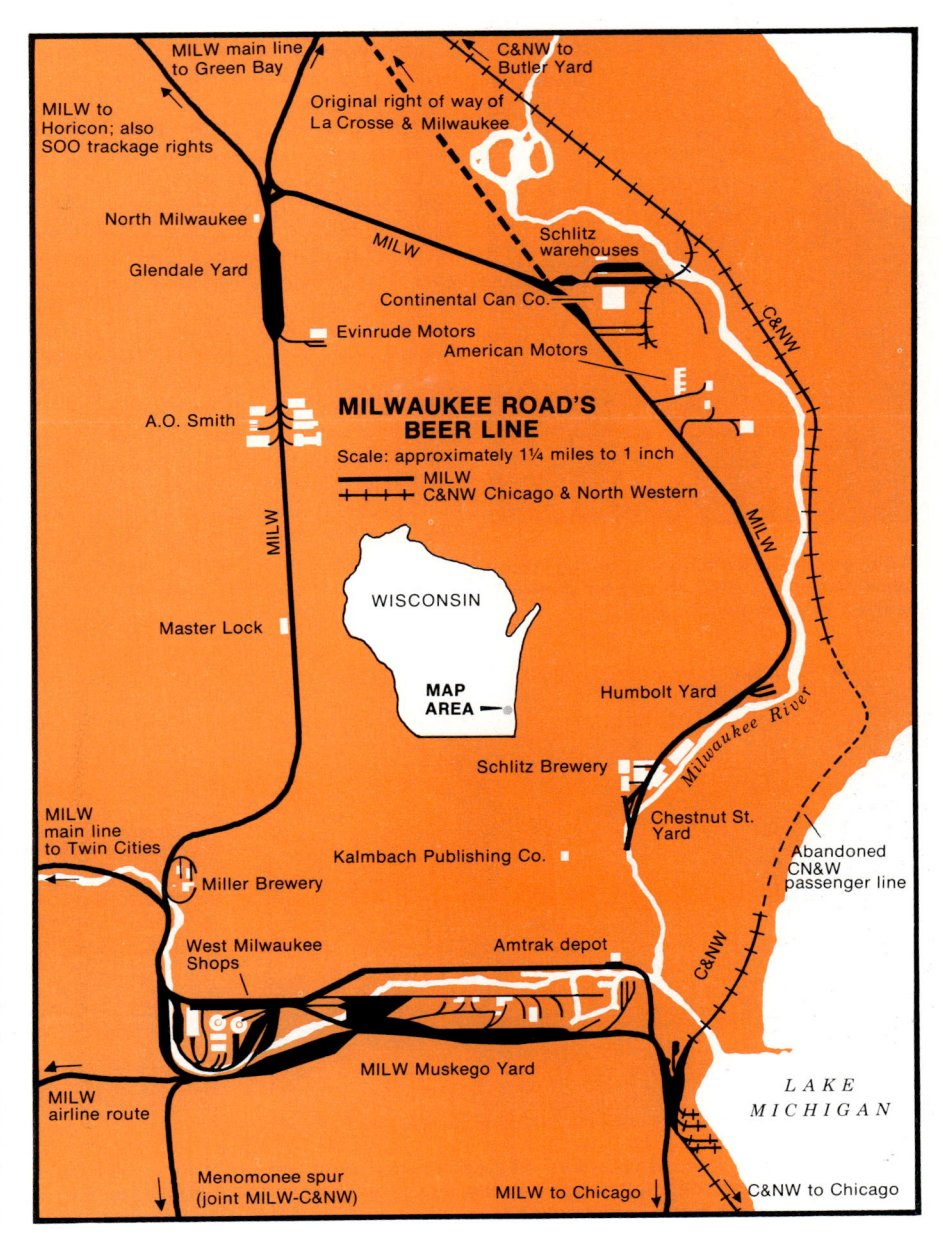

MILWAUKEE ROAD'S BEER LINE
Scale: approximately 1¼ miles to 1 inch
━━━━ MILW
┼┼┼┼ C&NW Chicago & North Western

47

Chestnut Street yard team tracks mark the south end of the Beer Line. Note the cement and asphalt platforms. Juneau Avenue — formerly Chestnut Street — cuts across the team tracks.

A new MILW MP15AC switches covered hoppers at upper Chestnut Street yard in the spring of 1977. The EMD MP's gradually replaced the FM's once so familiar to the Beer Line.

A closeup of the switchbacks on the "ramp track" (which is also shown on page 47) reveals retaining-wall detail.

main scenic feature of the layout, and they provide most of the switching opportunities. The grain plant receives corn syrup in tank cars and ships out spent grain in box cars. Baled hops arrive in refrigerator cars; some breweries use hops in pellet form, which are shipped in insulated box cars. Inbound malt arrives at the grain elevator in large covered hopper cars. Across Second Street is the bottling plant, which receives bottles and ships bottled beer in insulated, cushion-underframe box cars. The bottling plant also ships cullet (broken glass to be recycled) in a hopper car that is loaded through a chute that leads to the spur in Second Street. The Schlitz brewery uses natural gas for fuel but can burn oil in an emergency. Thus there's a reason for tank cars carrying oil on your model — or if you model an earlier era, hopper cars full of coal.

The other industries on our layout, the tannery and the sausage plant, let you operate several other types of cars. The tannery receives hides in old box cars (railroads reserve their lowest-grade box cars for hide service). The sausage factory (which in the prototype is adjacent to the Beer Line but not served by it) receives and ships products in meat reefers.

A brewery of earlier years will require an icing plant for the reefers in which draft beer is shipped. If the brewery operates its own fleet of cars, there's an excuse to have a small car-repair facility on the layout. Until recently the cars that Schlitz leased from Dairy Shippers Despatch (DSDX) were repaired on one of the tracks adjacent to the brewery.

The end of the layout has team tracks in one corner and a tavern in the other. (Milwaukee is a city of breweries and taverns — the classified section of the phone book devotes seven pages to taverns.) On the prototype the Pabst brewery uses the team tracks as its shipping and receiving point, carrying materials between the brewery and the team tracks in trucks. The team tracks can also be used by any other shipper or consignee who lacks a rail siding. Thus

Cullet — the glass of broken bottles — is gradually collected into a hopper to be forwarded to Chicago for recycling. It takes about one week to fill one hopper with cullet.

Pabst uses baled hops, which require the temperature protection afforded by mechanical reefers such as this. Schlitz uses pellet hops, which can be shipped in insulated box cars.

Below Holton Street viaduct the ramp track climbs northeasterly over a latticework trestle to return to mainline level. The lower track leads to non-brewery-related industries.

The 40-foot ice-activated reefers date this 1950's scene, looking northeast toward Holton Street viaduct from the ramp track. Note the trolley buses on the viaduct.

TRAINS: Wallace W. Abbey.

almost any type of car can be spotted on the team tracks. At the other end of our layout is a small freight platform where newsprint is unloaded for the city's two major dailies. On the prototype, wide-door box cars of Canadian National and its subsidiaries are the usual inhabitants of the newsprint track.

The Beer Line can provide operating enjoyment for one person or two — an engineer and a brakeman. The lower-level operating scheme is quite simple. The transfer freight arrives, its locomotive retreats to the engine track, and the switcher then sorts the cars on the tracks of the yard. The switcher puts the bay-window caboose of the transfer freight out of the way, picks up a privy-on-a-flat car switching caboose, couples to the train, and climbs the hill.

Switching on our layout takes a little time. Spurs point in both directions, and the grain elevator requires a switch-back move. Moreover, outbound cars already occupy those spurs, and there is very little space to store them. Your switcher may have to make another trip or two back to the yard before the work is done.

Variations on a theme

It is only a short step from the Milwaukee Road's Beer Line to a two-company theme: a line-haul railroad and a switching line. All you have to do, basically, is letter the two locomotives differently. For example, you can keep the F units (the prototype Beer Line transfer freight was powered by pairs of FP7's that once pulled *Hiawathas*) in Milwaukee Road colors and letter the switcher for a fictitious switching line such as Chestnut Street Terminal or Belt Railway of East Walnut Street.

The concept of an industry with lots of switching as part of a large layout also works well. Our Beer Belt Line track plan is patterned after this idea, and models a brewery located on a full-fledge main line. The double-track main is elevated to eliminate grade crossings, and it happens to separate the main part of the brewery from the bottling plant, just as the prototype Schlitz bot-

If your track is on different levels in the terminal switching areas, provide a shortcut like this for switchmen.

The yard office for Humboldt Yard fronts Humboldt Avenue south of the Beer Line grade crossing. This sturdy little structure would be a good prototype for a scratchbuilding project.

Grain-filled hoppers are weighed at the scale track in Chestnut Street yard. You could build a scaled-down version of the scale house in an evening or two in the workshop.

49

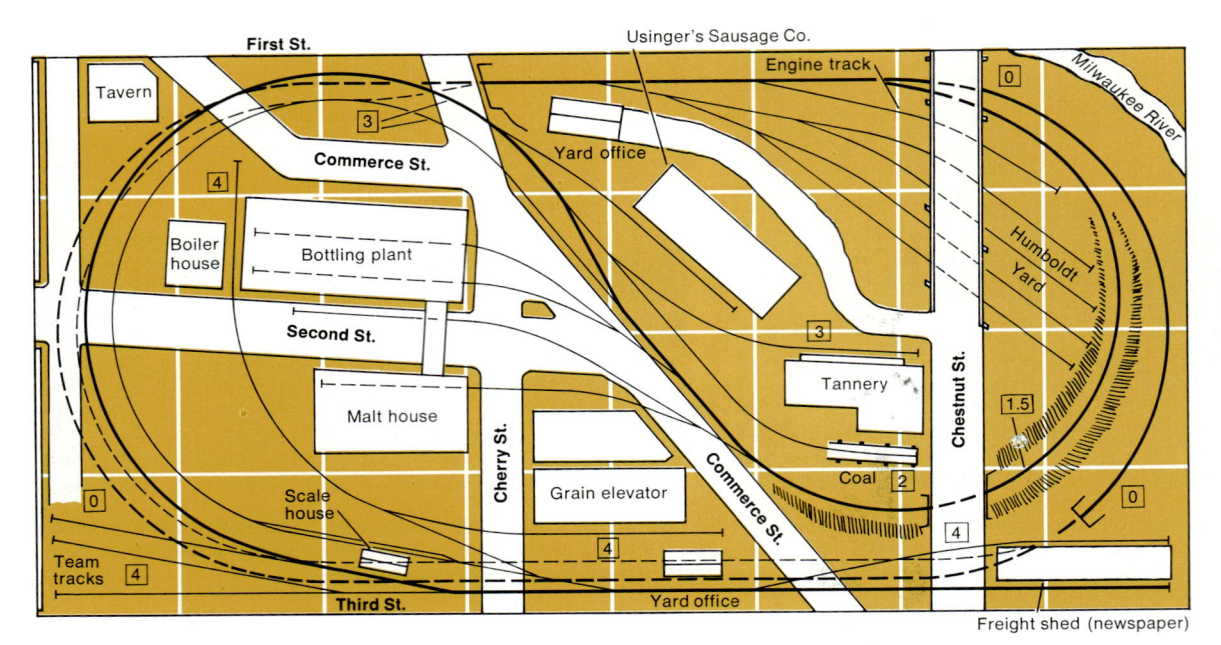

MILWAUKEE ROAD'S BEER LINE

Scale modeled		Z	N	TT	HO	S	O
Spacing of rulings	in.	4.50	6.00	9.00	12.00	18.00	24.00
Space horizontally	ft.-in.	3-0	4-0	6-0	8-0	12-0	16-0
Space vertically	ft.-in.	1-6	2-0	3-0	4-0	6-0	8-0
Minimum radius	in.	6.75	9.00	13.50	18.00	27.00	36.00
Parallel straight track spacing	in.	.71	.98	1.31	1.80	2.45	3.26
Parallel curved track spacing	in.	.89	1.22	1.63	2.25	3.06	4.08
Multiply elevations by	in.	.40	.54	.73	1.00	1.36	1.81

Turnouts: No. 4 in all scales

Spacing of rulings	mm.	112.50	150.00	225.00	300.00	450.00	600.00
Space horizontally	m.	.90	1.20	1.80	2.40	3.60	4.80
Space vertically	m.	.45	.60	.90	1.20	1.80	2.40
Minimum radius	mm.	169.00	225.00	338.00	450.00	675.00	900.00
Parallel straight track spacing	mm.	18.00	24.00	33.00	45.00	61.00	82.00
Parallel curved track spacing	mm.	22.00	31.00	41.00	56.00	76.00	102.00
Multiply elevations by	mm.	10.00	14.00	18.00	25.00	34.00	45.00

So that all areas of a model railroad remain accessible, no portion of a layout should be more than 30" (75 cm.) from an aisleway or access opening. Thus, when constructing a layout to Railroad You Can Model track-plan dimensions in a scale larger than HO, it may be necessary to add access openings or lift-out scenery sections where not already shown.

BEER BELT LINE

Scale modeled		Z	N	TT	HO	S	O
Spacing of rulings	in.	4.50	6.00	9.00	12.00	18.00	24.00
Space horizontally	ft.-in.	3-9	5-0	7-6	10-0	15-0	20-0
Space vertically	ft.-in.	0-9	1-0	1-06	2-0	3-0	4-0
Minimum radius	in.	11.25	15.00	22.50	30.00	45.00	60.00
Parallel straight track spacing	in.	.71	.98	1.31	1.80	2.45	3.26
Parallel curved track spacing	in.	.99	1.36	1.81	2.50	3.40	4.53
Multiply elevations by	in.	.40	.54	.73	1.00	1.36	1.81

Turnouts: unless otherwise indicated, No. 4 in all scales

Spacing of rulings	mm.	112.50	150.00	225.00	300.00	450.00	600.00
Space horizontally	m.	1.13	1.50	2.25	3.00	4.50	6.00
Space vertically	m.	.23	.30	.45	.60	.90	1.20
Minimum radius	mm.	281.00	375.00	563.00	750.00	1125.00	1500.00
Parallel straight track spacing	mm.	18.00	24.00	33.00	45.00	61.00	82.00
Parallel curved track spacing	mm.	25.00	34.00	45.00	63.00	85.00	113.00
Multiply elevations by	mm.	10.00	14.00	18.00	25.00	34.00	45.00

So that all areas of a model railroad remain accessible, no portion of a layout should be more than 30" (75 cm.) from an aisleway or access opening. Thus, when constructing a layout to Railroad You Can Model track-plan dimensions in a scale larger than HO, it may be necessary to add access openings or lift-out scenery sections where not already shown.

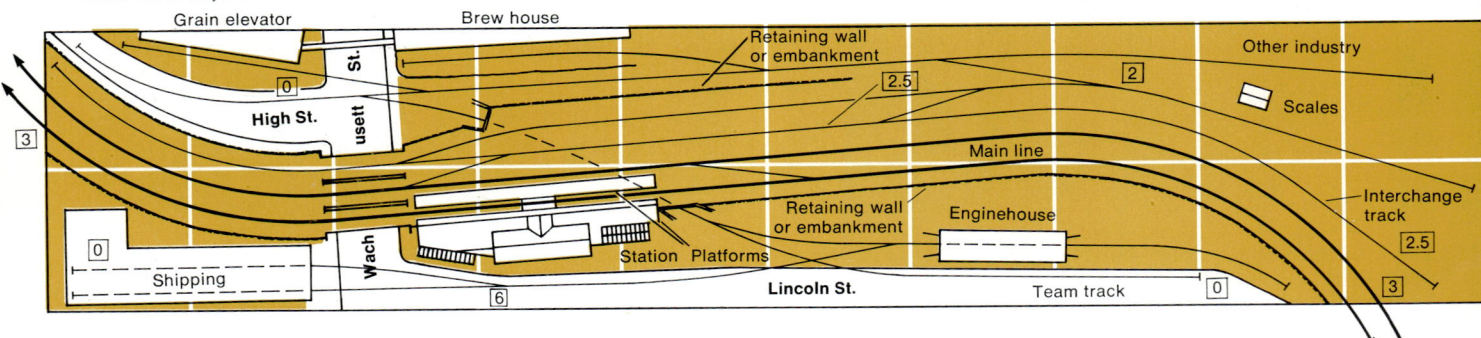

(Left) Humboldt Yard's modest terminal facilities include layover tracks, section-car sheds, and servicing tracks for locomotives and transfer cabooses. (Above) FP7's work transfers between downtown and Humboldt, laying over at Humboldt between runs.

Both photos, KALMBACH BOOKS: George Drury.

Malt destined for Pabst arrives at this facility across from Schlitz elevators. 
KALMBACH BOOKS: George Drury.

Standard grade-crossing flashers warn motorists of switching movements. 
KALMBACH BOOKS: Mike Schafer.

(Left) Trestle ramp track under Holton Street has planked trackway. (Above) Switchstand for scale track at Chestnut Street yard sits in a notch in the platform. 
KALMBACH BOOKS: George Drury.

Bumper for stub track in the street is painted in stripes to alert unwary motorists.
KALMBACH BOOKS: George Drury.

TRAINS: Wallace W. Abbey.

tling plant is across the tracks and a street from the rest of the brewery.

In the model this separation provides scenic interest and causes some complicated maneuvering on the part of the switcher. We justify the separation by saying that when the brewery expanded, the only space available for construction was on the other side of the tracks, necessitating underground conveyors and an underpass.

The model BBL is owned by the brewery, but it also serves one or two other industries in the neighborhood. The line owns one locomotive. Depending on your preference it can be a small steam switcher (conventional or fireless), a diesel, or even an electric, if you would like to string trolley wire. The engine deserves a name — Tarzan, Big Mo, Powerful Katrinka, or such. The engine spends the night in a one-stall run-through enginehouse down on the lower tail track. The building isn't a service facility; it is simply a place to keep the engine warm and out of the weather.

Space is tight, and several switchbacks are necessary to get a car from the bottling plant to the interchange track. The tail tracks limit the number of cars that can be handled more than the grades do. (An Athearn HO scale EMD switcher can pull two freight cars up a 10

51

Cars used by breweries

Era	Pre-prohibition	1940's	1950's/1960's	1970's
Inbound				
Malt, barley, and rice	36-foot wood box cars	40-foot wood box cars	40-foot steel box cars	Covered hoppers
Hops	36-foot wood reefers	40-foot wood reefers	40-foot steel reefers	Mechanical reefers and RBL's*
Corn grits	Not used	Not used	40-foot steel box cars	40-foot steel box cars and covered hoppers
Corn syrup	Not used	Not used	Not used	8000-, 10,000-, and 16,000-gallon tank cars
Coal	Wood hoppers	Wood and steel hoppers	Steel hoppers	Not used
Oil	Not used	Tank cars	Tank cars	Tank cars and trucks
New bottles, caps, and kegs	36-foot wood box cars	40-foot wood box cars	50-foot steel box cars	(Trucks)
Cans	Not used	40-foot wood box cars	(Trucks)	(Trucks)
Reusable kegs and bottles	These items are returned from wholesalers in the cars that brought the beer.			
Outbound				
Beer	36-foot wood reefers and box cars (15 tons)	40-foot wood reefers and box cars (20 tons)	40-foot steel reefers and box cars (30 tons)	50- and 60-foot RBL's (40-80 tons)
Spent grain	36-foot wood box cars	40-foot wood box cars	40-foot steel box cars	40- and 50-foot steel box cars and trucks
Crushed cans	Not used	36-foot gondolas	40-foot gondolas	40-foot gondolas
Cullet	Hopper cars	Hopper cars	Hopper cars	Hopper cars

*Refrigerator cars that carried beer were owned by the railroad, the breweries, and refrigerator-car companies. The RBL's (insulated plug-door box cars with load dividers) presently used are usually supplied to the railroads participating in the traffic. RBL's sometimes are called bunkerless refrigerator cars. Take away the cooling facilities from a refrigerator car and you have a box car.

---

per cent grade without much difficulty.) The BBL should be wired separately from the main line, but the interchange track should be wired so that it can be activated from either the mainline control panel or the BBL panel. Thus during an operating session you can indulge in two mutually exclusive pleasures — switching and just plain running trains.

The "Pabst Shipping Center" building (circle) is a clue that most cars in upper Chestnut Street yard are for Pabst.

All photos, KALMBACH BOOKS: George Drury.

All that brew needs a retail outlet, so don't forget to model a corner tavern or two. This one's called the Down Hill Bar.

Corn syrup arrives on the left track and spent grain is shipped from the right track at the prototype Schlitz plant. Today's larger cars overhang the loading/unloading area; danger signs warn passers-by not to tamper with couplers and brake apparatus. An enclosed dock facility would be effective for a model brewery because we usually can't model actual unloading activity.

52

Looking more European than North American, two WP&Y General Electric cab units wind their way south through Bennett, B. C., with train No. 2. The custom-built units were equipped with plows, but nose design also helped in snow-clearing.

Lawrence Treiman.

White Pass & Yukon

This narrow-gauge prototype has the qualities of a model railroad: sharp curves; short trains; and abrupt changes in scenery

Water-to-rail transfer facilities for freight and passengers offer modelers a chance to break away from modeling the conventional "landlocked" railroad. This is Skagway.

F. L. Jacques.

Both photos, Carl E. Mulvihill.

The WP&Y is blessed with great quantities of winter snow. (Above) White Pass section house, winter of 1961-62. (Below) Standard-gauge-width rotary at Fraser's loop.

53

Carcross (formerly Caribou Crossing), Yukon, was abundant with modeling possibilities when these three scenes were photographed in the 1950's. (Above left) Oil-burning 2-8-2 No. 81 pauses near Carcross water tank with mixed train No. 6. The wood cross sign warns snowplows of the impending grade crossing. (Above right) The water tank sits on a trestle adjacent to the wood swing bridge. Water tanks were enclosed and heated to prevent freeze-up. (Below) Steamer Tutshi, now retired, awaits tourists.

All photos, F. L. Jacques.

AT BEST a model railroad is a caricature of a conventional prototype railroad. On the model the curves are too sharp, the trains and the main line are too short, and the changes in scenery from one section to another are abrupt. Truth may be stranger than fiction, however, so perhaps you should look for a prototype road with features more like a model railroad than a real railroad. You may come closer to reality than by dreaming up a wholly fictional track plan of a more conventional railroad, and you can answer the skeptic who says, "You mean there's a prototype for *that*?"

Such a railroad is the White Pass & Yukon, a 3-foot-gauge line still very much in business between Skagway, Alaska, and Whitehorse, Yukon Territory. Its curves are too sharp (16 to 24 degrees); a 3.9 per cent ruling grade keeps its trains short; its surrounding scenery is space-savingly vertical and changes character with modellike abruptness in crossing timberline twice in a few miles. Yet it is a real railroad that has recently established a number of innovations in the handling of containerized freight.

History

The White Pass & Yukon Railway was started in 1898 at the height of the Yukon gold rush with the intention of laying track from Skagway to Fort Selkirk on the Yukon River, 325 miles. Construction began from Skagway and Whitehorse, and the gold spike was driven at Carcross, Yukon, on July 29, 1900. The WP&Y was not a railroad itself but an operating company. The railroads themselves were the Pacific & Arctic Railway & Navigation Co. (Alaska, 20.4 miles), the British Columbia-Yukon Railway (British Columbia, 32.2 miles), and the British Yukon Railway (Yukon Territory, 58.1 miles).

The WP&Y prospered for a few years, and it entered the Yukon River steamboat business. Then gold mining slackened. The railway ceased to pay dividends after 1913, and reorganization was necessary in 1918. For the next 20 years the WP&Y hung on by sheer determination.

The approach of World War II stirred the economy of the Yukon. The railway ordered a pair of 2-8-2's from Baldwin, and in 1937 it sponsored air services with a Ford Tri-Motor. Then in 1941 the bombing of Pearl Harbor triggered the construction of the Alaska Highway. One of the jump-off sites for construction crews was Whitehorse, at the north end of the WP&Y.

The White Pass was not equal to the challenge of moving men, materials, and machinery, and the United States Army moved in to operate the railroad. The Army purchased motive power from several narrow-gauge lines in the U. S. Among the imported locomotives were some Rio Grande K-28-class 2-8-2's. In 1943 the White Pass handled the equivalent of 10 years' worth of prewar tonnage.

After World War II the WP&Y returned to its primary business of bringing the necessities of life into the Yukon and moving silver, lead, zinc, and other minerals out.

WP&Y's resources for handling the cargoes now include not only the railroad but a container ship that shuttles between Vancouver, B. C., and Skagway, a 4-inch pipeline that parallels the railroad, and trucks for service beyond Whitehorse.

Equipment

In the early 1950's, the White Pass depended on three classes of modern 2-8-2's (with frames between the wheels, as on standard-gauge engines), a venerable outside-frame Ten-Wheeler, and an outside-frame Consolidation. The yellow-and-green General Electric diesels, numbered 90-100, were delivered between 1954 and 1966. They weigh between 84 and 86 tons, and their six-cylinder Alco 251 engines produce between 800 and 900 h.p. The 10 Montreal-built DL535E's were delivered in 1969 and 1971. They weigh 105 tons and their six-cylinder 251 engines produce 1200 h.p. They look like standard-gauge Montreal-built M630's that weren't Sanforized.

The passenger rolling stock is distinctive, especially in its two-to-one ratio of parlor cars to coaches. The cars are short (about 48 feet long), low-slung, and well-maintained. Two baggage cars and two ex-Sumpter Valley combines have cupolas to eliminate the need for a caboose while still providing an observation point for crewmen.

Until the advent of containerization, the freight-car roster included all types of cars. Now only a handful of box cars and tank cars keep WP&Y's fleet from being composed entirely of flat cars.

Modeling notes

The WP&Y track plan condenses the most scenic and heavily traveled portion of the line, from Skagway to Car-

54

cross, into a generous HOn3* layout. The plan is a point-to-loop one. The rugged terrain results in a lot of railroading to handle even light traffic, so there is no need in the model to simulate heavy traffic by sending the same train scurrying repeatedly past the same point. By the time you get a tonnage train from Skagway to Carcross, you'll have seen some real action.

In the interest of scenic realism the plan has been worked out so that at no point is more than one section of the main line in sight. There is access to the track at all points, and there is a backdrop behind the main line everywhere it goes, but you do not have to duck under the layout to follow a train from one end of the line to the other. As in all compact track plans, sections of main line theoretically miles apart are actually close together, but this isn't disconcerting because the other sections are either on the opposite side of the backdrop or behind your back.

To see how the White Pass has been condensed, we can run through a day's operations as they might go on a pike following the actual road not only in track arrangement but in schedules and equipment as well.

For our example, we'll naturally pick a day in summer when a steamer up the Inside Passage from Vancouver or Seattle has brought a shipload of tourists to Skagway. Many of them are going to Bennett, Whitehorse, or the West Taku Arm, so an additional train is scheduled on ship days.

We find this train has been made up and backed right down to shipside from the yards. Skagway's population is less than 700, but it has *two* places from which passenger trains depart. The West Taku Arm special is doubleheaded, with a solid consist of wonderful wood, open-platform parlor cars, neat but not gaudy in Pullman green with gold lettering. Soon after the arrival of the ship, the special train chuffs (or burbles, depending on your inclinations in motive power) smartly out of town past the shops, a thin trail of coal smoke streaming from the stovepipe on each car in the crisp morning air.

Action now shifts to the "downtown" station, which is just that. Against the protests of the town burghers many years ago, the White Pass & Yukon succeeded in establishing squatter's rights for a single track down the center of the main drag, and here the daily mixed train for Whitehorse is made ready to leave. The street is still unpaved and the sidewalks are still wood. Most of Skagway consists of buildings dating from the era of the 1898 gold rush to the Klondike territory. Some are occupied, but many are empty and still in a fair state of preservation considering their untended years. "You can't get fire insurance here, so nothing ever burns down," is the explanation of one native.

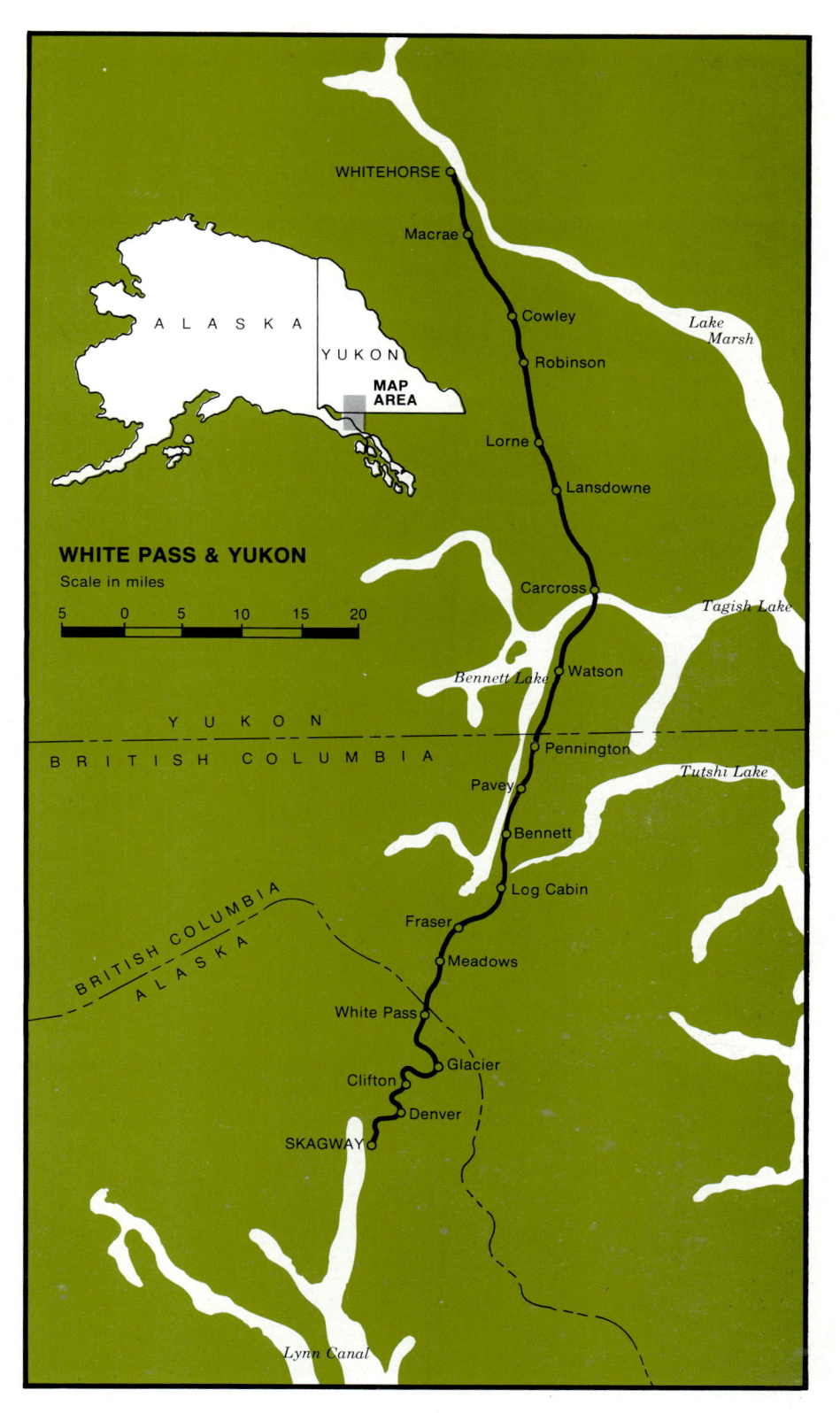

The Whitehorse train's passenger section, spotted at the station, consists of a flat car carrying two automobiles (there is no road out of Skagway), a baggage car with a caboose-style cupola perched atop its monitor roof, a coach, and a parlor car with observation end. The railing sports a round wood tail sign proclaiming "Gateway to the Yukon" in bright letters, but the sign is unlighted because the parlor cars operate only in the summer when at this latitude it never really gets dark. The locomotive is a modern if diminutive Mikado with large tender, front-end throttle, mechanical lubricators and other up-to-date appliances, plus a very carefully maintained air pump.

The train rolls out of the main street,

*HOn3 designates an HO scale model built in narrow gauge, in this case 3-foot gauge.

55

across a bridge, and up to the shops, where another locomotive is waiting on the main track in the middle of an assortment of loaded freight cars. The passenger section of the train couples onto the freight and a third engine (which in model practice might well be the helper from the preceding passenger train, just returned from the hill) is attached at the head end. The three engines highball off bravely but soon slow to a sedate pace of 12 to 15 mph as the 3.2 per cent-average grade takes hold.

Denver station is one of the easiest modeling jobs on record. It consists solely of a wood sign so inscribed, and that is all — period! A foot trail leads up to Denver glacier, an arm of the great Alaskan ice field up on the painted backdrop. Next comes Glacier, a similarly well-populated place at the end of a horseshoe curve, much of which is on a curved wood trestle. The climb continues, reaching a climax at Tunnel Mountain where a rock shelf blasted in the cliff, a trestle, a short rock tunnel, and a timber snowshed follow in quick succession.

The train then crosses Steel Bridge, an impressive structure flanked by two short, curved wooden trestles. The Montreal-built diesels were heavy

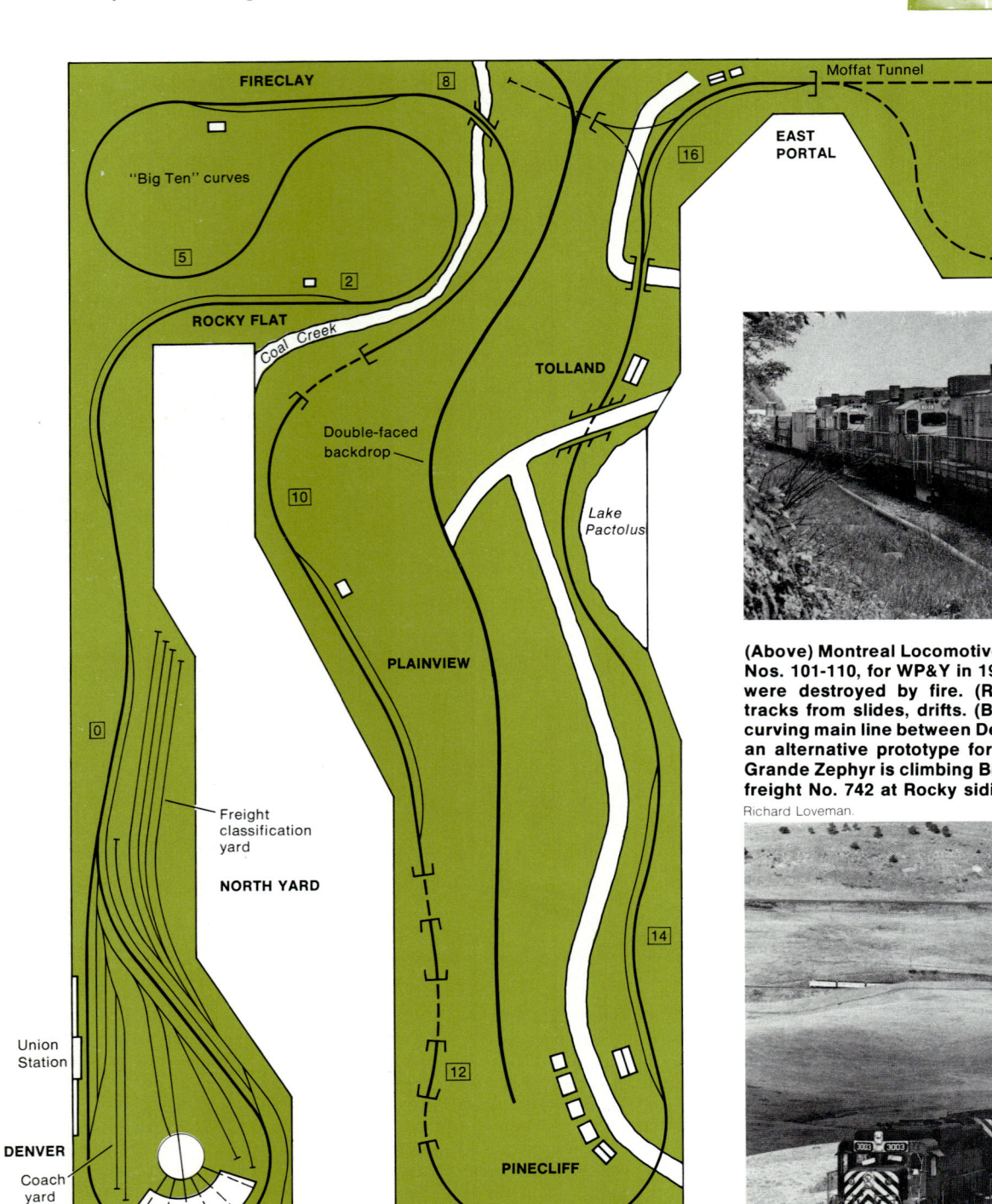

(Above) Montreal Locomotive Works built 10 DL535E's, Nos. 101-110, for WP&Y in 1969 and 1971; 101 and 105 were destroyed by fire. (Right) Snowsheds protect tracks from slides, drifts. (Below) D&RGW's climbing, curving main line between Denver and Moffat Tunnel is an alternative prototype for the WP&Y plan. The Rio Grande Zephyr is climbing Big Ten loops after meeting freight No. 742 at Rocky siding.

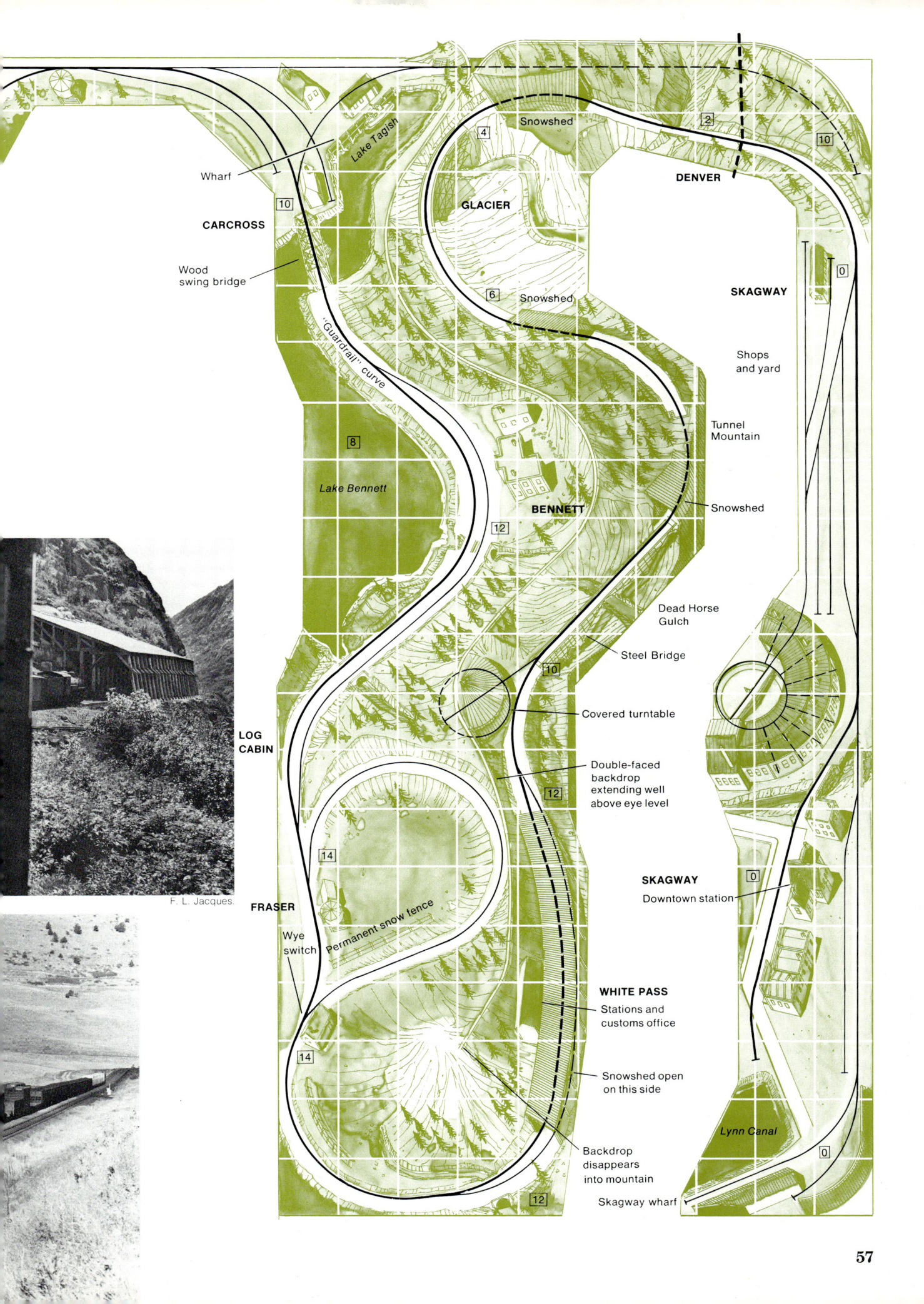

Wharf
Lake Tagish
Snowshed
[4]
[2]
[10]
CARCROSS
DENVER
[10]
GLACIER
SKAGWAY
Wood swing bridge
[6] Snowshed
[0]
"Guardrail" curve
Shops and yard
Tunnel Mountain
Snowshed
[8]
Lake Bennett
BENNETT
[12]
Dead Horse Gulch
Steel Bridge
[10]
Covered turntable
LOG CABIN
Double-faced backdrop extending well above eye level
[12]
[14]
FRASER
Wye switch
Permanent snow fence
SKAGWAY
Downtown station [0]
WHITE PASS
Stations and customs office
Snowshed open on this side
[14]
Lynn Canal
Backdrop disappears into mountain
[0]
[12]
Skagway wharf

F. L. Jacques

57

(Above) The covered turntable at the steel bridge near White Pass was for helpers. Before the bridge (below) was built in 1901, trains had to use a tortuous switchback up the side of Dead Horse Gulch. The new MLW diesels required replacement of the bridge.

Stove-heated parlor car Lake Dewey is sub-lettered "P.&A.R.&N.Co."

Scale modeled		Z	N	TT	HO	S	O
Spacing of rulings	in.	4.50	6.00	9.00	12.00	18.00	24.00
Space horizontally	ft.-in.	8-9	11-0	15-6	20-0	30-0	40-0
Space vertically	ft.-in.	7-6	10-0	15-0	20-0	30-0	40-0
Minimum radius	in.	6.00	8.00	12.00	16.00	24.00	32.00
Parallel straight track spacing	in.	.71	.98	1.31	1.80	2.45	3.26
Multiply elevations by	in.	.40	.54	.73	1.00	1.36	1.81

Turnouts: unless otherwise indicated, No. 4 in all scales

Spacing of rulings	mm.	112.50	150.00	225.00	300.00	450.00	600.00
Space horizontally	m.	2.63	3.30	4.65	6.00	9.00	12.00
Space vertically	m.	2.25	3.00	4.50	6.00	9.00	12.00
Minimum radius	mm.	150.00	200.00	300.00	400.00	600.00	800.00
Parallel straight track spacing	mm.	18.00	24.00	33.00	45.00	61.00	82.00
Multiply elevations by	mm.	10.00	14.00	18.00	25.00	34.00	45.00

Horizontal and vertical dimensions of this layout allow for a minimum aisleway width of 24". To maintain this minimum aisleway width when using TT or smaller scales, the layout should be expanded at the suggested location indicated by the dashed line.

So that all areas of a model railroad remain accessible, no portion of a layout should be more than 30" (75 cm.) from an aisleway or access opening. Thus, when constructing a layout to Railroad You Can Model track-plan dimensions in a scale larger than HO, it may be necessary to add access openings or lift-out scenery sections where not already shown.

enough to require replacement of the cantilever span with a simple girder affair; modeler's license can either strengthen your Steel Bridge or lighten your DL535E's. Steel Bridge carries the track high above Dead Horse Gulch, named for the thousands of pack animals that died on the slopes of the pass during the gold rush. At the upper end of the bridge is a covered turntable on a spur, and we also notice that the telegraph poles have been superseded by a cable lying on the ground along the track, recognition of the heavy snowfall along this section of the line.

At White Pass, the track levels off somewhat and enters a snowshed in which the station and Customs offices at the international boundary are located. While the Canadian officials are checking the passengers, the lead engine and first section of freight cars uncouple and pull ahead on the main, releasing the mid-train helper. It backs through the siding to the turntable at Steel Bridge where it is turned for the trip back to Skagway.

The remaining two engines take the train out of White Pass up a continuing grade to Fraser, where the lead engine takes water.

Log Cabin, highest point on the line, is where the second helper — the engine immediately ahead of the passenger cars — is taken out (using the south end of the Bennett siding as a spur track). It backs to Fraser and turns on the loop there for the return to Skagway. Fraser's loop is a necessity for handling the rotary plows in winter. The snow is frequently so deep that even the short backing move, which would be necessary in turning around on a wye, might not be possible.

At Bennett our train makes its lunch stop. Bennett consists solely of the station-restaurant and the ruins of a log church, started in the gold rush days when Bennett was the temporary terminus of the railroad, but never finished. For once it's practicable to model a lineside town in its entirety. About the time we finish lunch, a southbound train pulls in from Carcross, its empty parlor cars being deadheaded back to Skagway to meet tomorrow's ship. The passengers these cars carried to Carcross this morning are now enjoying a spectacular round trip to the West Taku Arm of Lake Tagish aboard the stern-wheeler *Tutshi*, and they will return to Skagway on the same cars tomorrow.

As the brakeman throws the switch to send the southbound train into the siding, we notice that the switch is of stub design (as are practically all switches on the WP&Y). Under the relatively light traffic stub switches stand up well enough, and they are much to be appreciated in winter since there is no crevice where the snow can collect and keep the points from closing. Since our

A businesslike, no-nonsense station building greets passengers arriving at Whitehorse. The 81 has just rolled in with mixed No. 1 from Skagway carrying an assortment (to say the least) of equipment that includes flatbeds of autos.

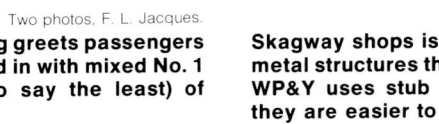

Two photos, F. L. Jacques.

Skagway shops is an interesting array of weathered wood and metal structures that would add character to any model railroad. WP&Y uses stub switches (switches without points) because they are easier to maintain in winter than regular switches.

train is considerably longer than the passing track, we stage a saw-by meet and then pull out for Carcross.

Next comes Guard Rail curve, sharpest on the main line, and then a quaint wood gallows-type swing bridge over the Lake Bennett outlet just as the line enters Carcross. This bridge is advertised as the most northerly movable bridge in the world. The train swings to the left at Carcross and there is for the first time since Skagway some switching of freight cars in and out of sidings and the wharf track.

Since the line from Carcross to Whitehorse is less spectacular, we have condensed this 50-mile stretch into an unscenicked loop. So in the model the train which just left Carcross comes back into view quickly enough to represent its own southbound sister mixed train on the prototype. On the return trip, it will stop for customs at White Pass and will make a few short stops at the most scenic points to allow the camera-carrying passengers to take pictures while the wheel treads and brake shoes cool down.

At the Skagway shops the passenger section of the train is left on the main between the yard switches. The engine then backs through the siding past the train and, leaving the freight cars on the main, pushes the passenger cars the rest of the way down to the station. (The passengers are in no great rush since the train has taken all day to cover only 110 miles.) The engine then switches the freight cars while the express unloads.

Let's see how the WP&Y scenes fit the confines of the layout. Steel Bridge won't be quite full scale, but it can still be awesome in comparison to the little trains that cross it. From Tunnel Mountain to Log Cabin the White Pass line is too high to be surrounded with any vegetation beyond low bushes. This is helpful in that the lack of trees makes many home pikes look as though they were above timberline anyway. Nearer Skagway the lower slopes are forested, but most of the trees can be painted on a backdrop and hence will be neither the problem nor the expense that they would be if actually modeled.

Lake Bennett is a modeler's dream. Fed by glacier water, it is a beautiful blue-green and quite opaque. The surrounding mountains temper the winds to the extent that the lake's surface frequently resembles a mirror's. Extra space for the lake's waters has been provided in this plan so that, by representing the lake with smooth glass painted on the underside, the model trains and their reflections can be viewed rolling along. It would make a sight to behold, and one that is rarely modeled, too.

One thing missing on the real WP&Y is lineside industry. Carcross has only a small tie-treating plant, and, aside from the steamer wharves there and at Skagway and Whitehorse, that's all. This shouldn't stop you from adding a few mines — there's plenty of fool's gold, at least, in them thar hills.

The heated roundhouse at Skagway is a multistall affair because virtually all the equipment needed to run the twice-weekly winter schedule must be kept indoors between trips. Even though operations with simulated snow and a working rotary plow are not feasible, you'll want to have a rotary in the house along with the superintendent's rail jeep and other miscellaneous equipment.

How about standard gauge?

The White Pass track plan could be used almost as is in N scale for a model of a standard-gauge, heavy-duty mountain railroad. The 24-inch curves, while broad for N scale, would add greatly to the illusion of a heavy railroad. For a specific example, let's choose the Denver & Rio Grande Western from Denver, Colo., up to the East Portal of the Moffat Tunnel. Like the White Pass, the Rio Grande has a stiff climb through thinly populated country. The Rio Grande has heavier traffic, so add a few sidings, and don't omit the double bowknot of track called Big Ten between Rocky and Coal Creek. The yard and terminal facilities must be enlarged to convert Skagway to Denver's North Yard. A couple of holding tracks inside or beyond the Moffat Tunnel adds a capacity to the layout to help simulate the D&RGW's busy line — freights, local passenger trains, and the *California Zephyr*.

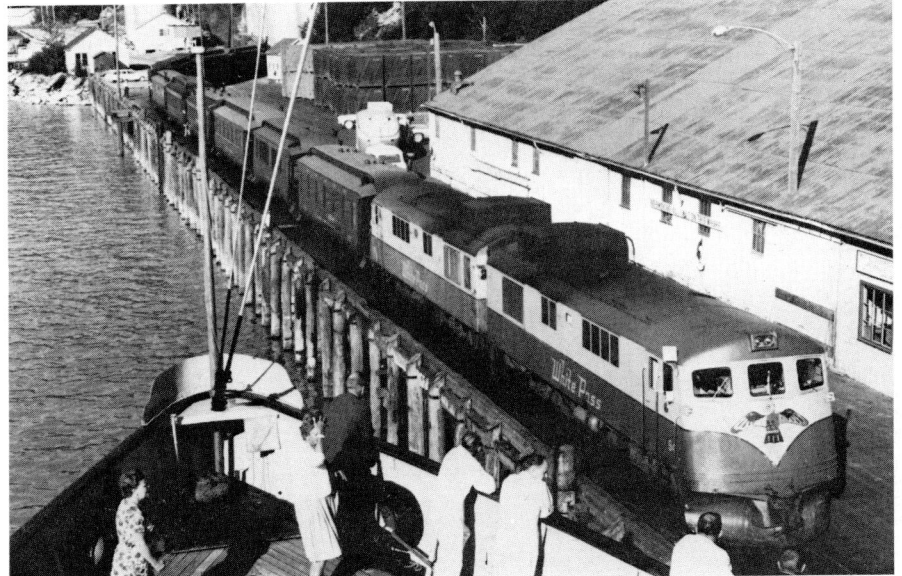

Carl E. Mulvihill.

A 14-car passenger extra delivers tourists to the boat at Skagway in August 1964.

Bendix Aviation Corp.

The longevity of Ma & Pa 4-4-0 No. 6 led to the acclaim that it was one of the last surviving examples of the American Standard wheel arrangement; No. 6 was built in 1901 and served into the 1950's. The Richmond Locomotive Works product is wheeling train 31 into Delta, Pa., probably in the 1940's.

Maryland & Pennsylvania

A classic short line, the "Ma & Pa" rambled 77 miles to connect two cities 54 miles apart

KALMBACH BOOKS: Mike Schafer.

Part of the fascination of the M&P even today are the old buildings, railroad and nonrailroad, along the right of way. This scene is at Muddy Creek Forks in 1974.

William Moedinger.

Baldwin-built 4-6-0 No. 27 puts on a good show with her baggage-mail car and coach. Short trains, interesting structures, and tight curves make the Ma & Pa ideal for modeling.

Ma & Pa 2-8-0 No. 43 chuffs dutifully across Gross trestle near Sharon in November 1955, thirty years after her birth, with one box car and a bobber caboose. The grade over the curved trestle sometimes required helpers. The dreamlike quality of this scene reminds us modelers that we can re-create a bit of Ma & Pa history even though the rails and trestle of this scene are long gone.

James P. Gallagher.

HERITAGE can be defined as something of value passed on to heirs. The prototype Maryland & Pennsylvania Railroad has left a rich heritage to model railroaders. Perhaps no other short line in the country has had such distinctive equipment, scenery, structures, and overall appeal for a railroad you could model. Prof. George W. Hilton, author of *The Ma & Pa – A History of the Maryland & Pennsylvania Railroad* (Howell-North, 1963), once said that the road "might have come from the mind of some Velasquez or Rembrandt among model railroaders who, having exhausted his art in HO and O gauges, finally came to the hills north of Baltimore to create his masterpiece at a scale of 12 inches to the foot."

Actually, the Ma & Pa was created by the merger of two former narrow-gauge lines, the York & Peachbottom in Pennsylvania and the Maryland Central in Maryland. They were merged in 1891 to form the Baltimore & Lehigh, which went bankrupt in 1893. The Pennsylvania portion of the B&L was reorganized as the York Southern; the Maryland trackage also was reorganized but retained the name Baltimore & Lehigh. Between 1893 and 1901, both roads converted to standard gauge and on February 12, 1901,

MARYLAND & PENNSYLVANIA   Prior to 1958

For northbound trains this through truss bridge over Winters Run was a gateway to the tiny hamlet of Vale, Md.

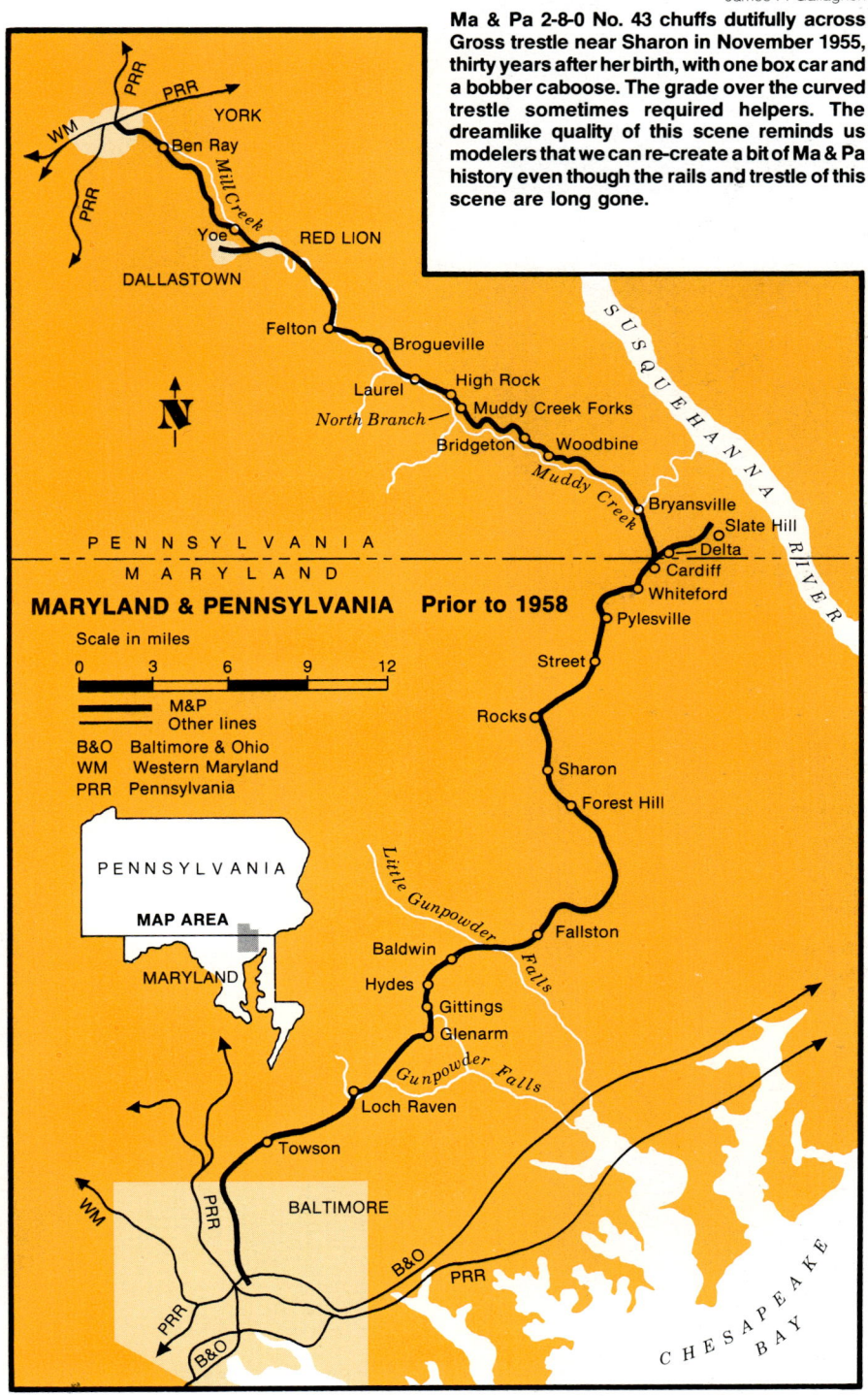

Eldon A. Behr.

61

(Above left) SW9 No. 82 idles at the York enginehouse in 1974. The 82 had the dubious honor of hauling the last train on the Maryland Division. (Above right) Baldwin 0-6-0 No. 29 is being turned at Baltimore in 1952. (Below) Motor car 62 was built by St. Louis Car and powered by an Electro-Motive distillate engine.

Like many railroads, M&P began to dieselize soon after World War II. The 70, here at York in 1947, was an SW1 built in 1946.

M&P 86 is an ex-Reading GP7 that was purchased along with two other diesels to fulfill duties on an expanded Ma & Pa.

A 1925 builder photo of No. 43 reveals the 2-8-0's stout proportions. The 43 was the last steam power bought by M&P. M&P never owned an engine with trailing wheels.

merged to form the Maryland & Pennsylvania. The road operated through the rugged, agriculturally rich countryside that lay between Baltimore, Md., and York, Pa., with a 2-mile branch between Delta and Slate Hill, Pa., and a mile-long branch between Dallastown Junction and Dallastown, Pa.

The Ma & Pa took the long way around to get from York to Baltimore. The distance between the two cities is roughly 54 miles, but the Ma & Pa rambled 77.2 miles to join them. This roundabout route was a heritage that the former narrow-gauge components left to the Ma & Pa, and is one reason the road remained essentially a country-style short line beloved by fans and offering so much for model railroaders.

The Ma & Pa of today proves that fact can be stranger than fiction. In 1958 all trackage south of Whiteford, Md., was abandoned, cutting Ma & Pa's route-miles from 77.2 to 34.8. However, by 1977 the road had more than 85 route-miles—the most ever in its colorful history. Such a turnabout in size is somewhat unusual for a short line; ironically, the Ma & Pa's sudden growth was a result of one of the largest railroad mergers in American history.

Consolidated Rail Corporation's formation on April 1, 1976, had a profound effect on several railroads, including some not involved directly in the merger. A number of rail lines belonging to the CR member roads became orphaned after the merger date. These surplus lines were either abandoned or taken over by other railroads. M&P "adopted" a portion of one of these orphan lines—the York-Walkersville (Md.) segment of Penn Central's (ex-Pennsylvania) branch to Frederick, Md. The road also purchased some industrial trackage in York from the PC. These additions increased M&P's mileage by more than 50 miles. This chapter will focus on the original Ma & Pa lines, however.

Livelihood of the Ma & Pa

Before World War I, the Ma & Pa handled large amounts of local and l.c.l. (less-than-carload) freight — farm produce, cattle, and milk from the nearby farms, slate and marble from the nearby quarries, and cigars, cigar boxes, and furniture from the Red Lion district. The Ma & Pa could not depend on through freight for its livelihood because York and Baltimore already were joined by two railroads, the Pennsylvania and the Western Maryland. PRR's and WM's shorter, faster routes between the two cities and the lack of connections with any railroads but PRR, WM, and WM's parent Baltimore & Ohio precluded the Ma & Pa's becoming a bridge route.

In addition to l.c.l. business, thousands of passengers were handled every year — farmers, commuters, salesmen, and townsfolk. Indeed, passengers, mail, express, and a large amount of milk business (one of Ma & Pa's passenger runs was nicknamed "The Milky Way") accounted for 50 per cent of total revenues. At least two daily through passenger trains each way operated between York and Baltimore, with numerous commuter trains operating between Bel Air, Md., and Baltimore. There was also a modest commuter operation between Delta and York.

After the war, the nature of Ma & Pa's business changed quickly. Passenger, milk, and l.c.l. traffic declined, but new industries sprang up along the route of the Ma & Pa, industries large enough to supply full carload freight. In later years, slate (in granule form for roofing) accounted for 58 per cent of the freight revenue of the Ma & Pa, with most of it coming from the Delta-Cardiff-Whiteford area. There was also a modest amount of coal traffic and service to and from quarries, especially around Cardiff where green marble was quarried. After truck competition contributed to the demise of l.c.l. business, interchange carload freight traffic became the mainstay of the Maryland & Pennsylvania. In Baltimore the Ma & Pa had interchanged directly with the Baltimore & Ohio and the Pennsylvania railroads. The Ma & Pa also had indirect interchange with the Baltimore & Annapolis (an electric line) and the Western Maryland. In York, Ma & Pa connected with the Pennsylvania (later Penn Central and then Conrail) and with the Western Maryland (later a part of Chessie System).

Today, the primary function of the M&P is to serve industries in the York and Hanover (Pa.) areas daily. Other points are served two or three times a week or as needed.

Equipment and operations

For a line only 77 miles long, the Ma & Pa had an interesting assortment of motive power, especially steam. Over the years the road operated 4-4-0's, 4-6-0's, two sizes of 2-8-0's, and 0-6-0 switchers.

Passenger service was handled by the 4-4-0's or the dual-service 4-6-0's. The usual consist of the *Baltimore Mail* and the *York Mail* was one of Ma & Pa's highly distinctive baggage-mail cars and an open-platform coach. Gas-electrics Nos. 61 and 62, built by Electro-Motive Corporation, made their appearances in 1927 and 1928 respectively to take over passenger service. They were straight coach-type cars, and they hauled a baggage-mail trailer behind them. The two gas-electrics each made a round trip daily between York and Baltimore, except on Sundays when only the gas-electric stationed at York made a round trip. Running time between the two cities was over 4 hours,

Bruce D. Fales.
Open-vestibule wood coach No. 20 was built for the Ma & Pa by American Car & Foundry in 1913. By 1958 the 20 had migrated north to the Strasburg Railroad.

J. Lawrence Dixon.
Bobber caboose 2005, built in 1889, was bought from the Pittsburgh & Lake Erie.

William Moedinger.
M&P banned wood box cars like No. 729 from interchange service after 1937.

J. Lawrence Dixon.
Windowed tool car X3 was photographed in Baltimore in November 1941.

Bruce D. Fales.
Caboose 2002 was built by the Ma & Pa in 1905; a side door was added in 1961.

William Moedinger.
Few short lines can boast having a complete set of wrecker equipment, but in 1940 photographer Moedinger recorded M&P derrick X1 and idler X2 at Baltimore. Derricks were a mighty handy thing to have around on a railroad that was 50 per cent curves.

63

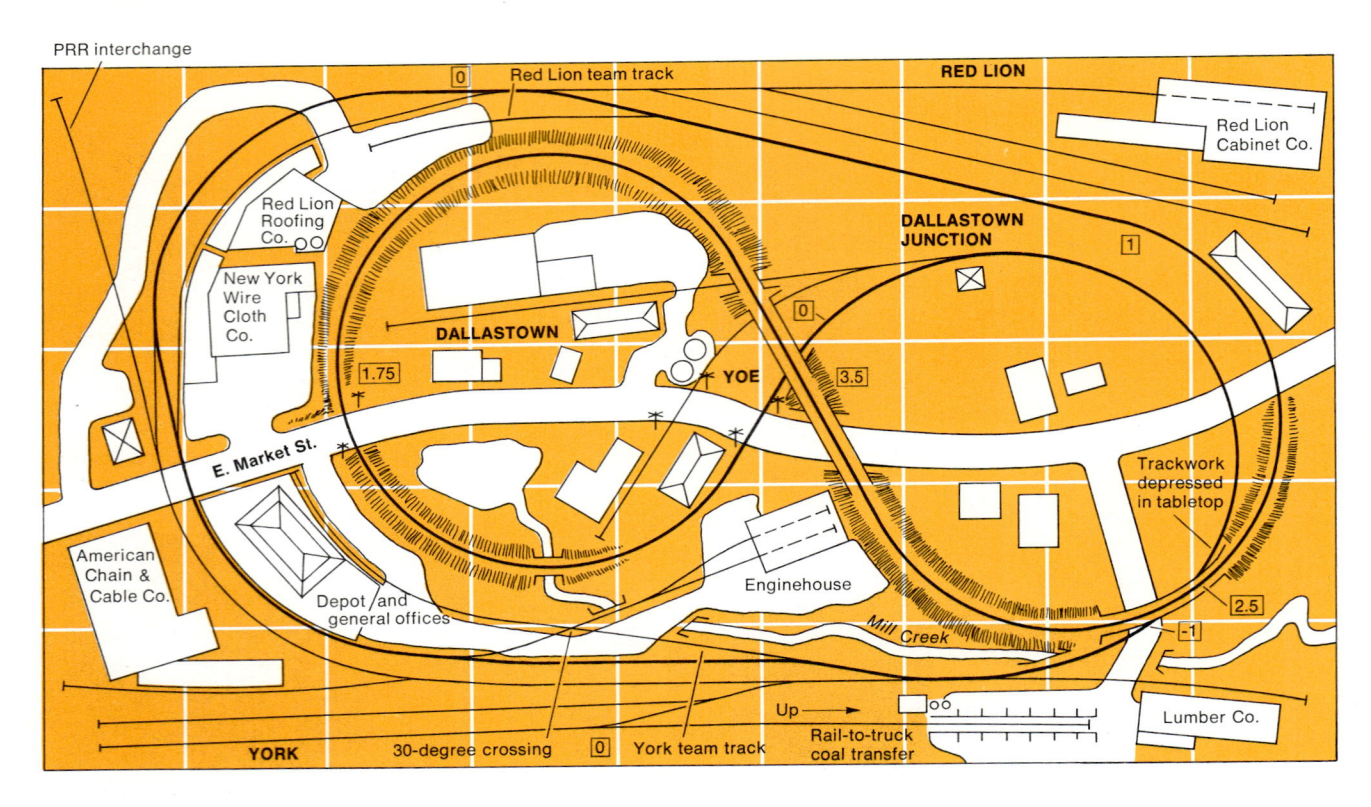

Scale modeled		Z	N	TT	HO	S	O
Spacing of rulings	in.	4.50	6.00	9.00	12.00	18.00	24.00
Space horizontally	ft.-in.	3-5	4-6	6-9	9-0	13-6	18-0
Space vertically	ft.-in.	1-11	2-6	3-9	5-0	7-6	10-0
Minimum radius	in.	6.75	9.00	13.50	18.00	27.00	36.00
Parallel straight track spacing	in.	.71	.98	1.31	1.80	2.45	3.26
Parallel curved track spacing	in.	1.38	1.90	2.54	3.50	4.76	6.34
Multiply elevations by		.40	.54	.73	1.00	1.36	1.81
Turnouts: No. 4 in all scales							
Spacing of rulings	mm.	112.50	150.00	225.00	300.00	450.00	600.00
Space horizontally	m.	1.01	1.35	2.03	2.70	4.05	5.40
Space vertically	m.	.56	.75	1.13	1.50	2.25	3.00
Minimum radius	mm.	169.00	225.00	338.00	450.00	675.00	900.00
Parallel straight track spacing	mm.	18.00	24.00	33.00	45.00	61.00	82.00
Parallel curved track spacing	mm.	35.00	48.00	63.00	88.00	119.00	159.00
Multiply elevations by	mm.	10.00	14.00	18.00	25.00	34.00	45.00

So that all areas of a model railroad remain accessible, no portion of a layout should be more than 30" (75 cm.) from an aisleway or access opening. Thus, when constructing a layout to Railroad You Can Model track-plan dimensions in a scale larger than HO, it may be necessary to add access openings or lift-out scenery sections where not already shown.

Sounding like a mainline manifest, the 42 thunders past Baldwin's shingle-sided depot in 1940.

William Moedinger.

Both photos, Eldon A. Behr.

As we mentioned earlier, structures are one of the high points to modeling the Ma & Pa, and there are many to choose from. (Above left) Fallston depot had upstairs living quarters that rated shuttered windows. Canopies were provided for both rail and road loading platforms. (Above center) The small shelter and platform at Rocks had rather casual construction.

A 19-car train moving upgrade on Gross trestle. Weight restrictions required that the helper be placed 12 cars back so that only one engine at a time placed stress on the structure.

Two photos, William Moedinger.

Station scene at Bridgeton in 1940 shows a board-and-batten depot with large eaves and a stone foundation. Top of white post had high-water mark from last Muddy Creek flood.

with a trip up the Dallastown branch (in one direction backwards) thrown in for free. When one of the gas-electrics broke down or was in the shops, a 4-4-0 or 4-6-0 substituted. The motor cars lasted until 1954 when all passenger service was discontinued.

Although passenger consists were short, you could operate a railfan trip as an excuse to run long trains on your model Ma & Pa. The railroad was a pioneer in running railfan excursions, and has operated such trips with as many as 10 P-54-class suburban coaches borrowed from the Pennsylvania Railroad. Usually, one of the 4-6-0's handled fan trains, but at times a heavy 2-8-0 was used. Later, diesels hauled fan trips.

Light Consolidations (2-8-0's) handled most of the regularly scheduled freight runs until 1914 when two heavy Consolidations — Nos. 41 and 42 — were purchased. Later, a third heavy 2-8-0 was purchased, the 43. These three 2-8-0's, with their short frames, small drivers, and high tractive effort, were built to negotiate the sharp curves and steep grades of the Ma & Pa.

Shortly after the end of World War II, Ma & Pa management saw a need for new locomotives. Steam was considered, but dieselization proved to be a more economically sound investment. In 1946 Electro-Motive built three locomotives for the Ma & Pa: No. 70, a 600-h.p. SW1; and Nos. 80 and 81, 1000-h.p. NW2's. A fourth diesel, No. 82, an EMD 1200-h.p. SW9, arrived in 1951.

Although the diesels were intended for freight service, they often substituted for the motor cars on weekend passenger runs because the diesels were cheaper to operate. When the line was cut back to Whiteford in 1958, the Ma & Pa found itself with a surplus of motive power, so in 1959 the 70 and 80 were sold to Republic Steel in Canton, Ohio. However, by 1968 the Ma & Pa needed more diesels and in that year purchased an SW900 from the Steelton & Highspire, another Pennsylvania short line, and numbered it 83. The addition of the Walkersville line in 1976 resulted in still another need for more motive power, so the road acquired an SW9 from the Pittsburgh & Lake Erie and an NW2 and a GP7, both of them ex-Reading. M&P numbered the three additions 84, 85, and 86 respectively.

Freight equipment was, of course, mostly that of railroads with which the Ma & Pa exchanged traffic, although the road did own box cars, gondolas, and milk refrigerators. As the years went by, Ma & Pa's antiquated equipment was restricted to home property by interchange regulations. Much of it eventually was converted to maintenance-of-way equipment. The company also maintained a complete work train. The rebuilt steel box cars Ma & Pa now owns are painted black; box cars delivered new are blue. Both new and rebuilt cars sport a yellow emblem that boasts "The famous Ma & Pa." Before Ma & Pa ended caboose operations, it owned three four-wheel bobbers, Nos. 2003 and 2004 (ex-Kanawha & Michigan), and 2006 (ex-Pennsylvania). It also had an eight-wheel caboose, the 2002.

Three photos, KALMBACH BOOKS: Mike Schafer.

(Above left) A 1974 view of Felton shows that the tracks pass through town without much fanfare. (Above center) Concrete post at York marked start of M&P trackage. (Above right) The red brick station at Red Lion has a wood canopy supported by steel columns. A concrete platform faces the curved main line and a wood sign on the roof denotes depot owner.

In various Eastern towns it was customary to build some houses and stores facing the tracks rather than the street. Yoe residents living in these well-kept frame houses have a fine view of the Ma & Pa. Even the market sign is off-street.

Up and down the right of way

The topography between York and Baltimore makes a profile of the Ma & Pa look like a roller coaster. For instance, the right of way between Baltimore and Delta (43.8 miles) ascended and descended 10 summits on grades ranging from 1.4 per cent to 3.3 per cent. From Delta north, the railroad descends to 225 feet above sea level, rises to 900 feet at Red Lion, then descends 500 feet into York. The ruling grade on this 33.4-mile section is 2.5 per cent and the many sharp curves were intended to accommodate only narrow-gauge equipment. As a matter of fact, on Ma & Pa fan trips the only off-line passenger cars that could be used were PRR's 54-foot suburban coaches; longer cars would snag in some of the rock cuts on curves.

Thirty-six miles of the 77-mile main line — approximately 47 per cent of the main line — was on curves. There were 476 curves, 55 of them ranging in sharpness between 16 and 20 degrees (most railroads rarely have curves exceeding 6 degrees). As a contrast, curves on the Denver & Rio Grande Western Railroad, which has some of the toughest stretches of mainline railroading in the United States, do not exceed 12 degrees. Some of the curves on the Ma & Pa are so sharp they require guardrails.

Don't these problems of curves and grades sound similar to those model railroaders face?

Prior to the abandonment of Maryland trackage in 1958, the Ma & Pa had 114 bridges, with a combined length of 11,155 feet. The majority of them were wooden trestles. In many places the Ma & Pa used trestles instead of fills to cross small valleys. When the Ma & Pa purchased its two heavy Consolidations, the wooden bridges had to be reinforced with steel I-beams.

Before the line was cut back to Whiteford, the main shops and car storage yards were in Baltimore. The facilities at York were sufficient only for servicing the two locomotives permanently in service at that end of the line. One of the 0-6-0 yard goats and one of the light Consolidations handled all yard and interchange work in York. A 4-4-0 was stored in the enginehouse to substitute for the gas-electric car in case of an emergency.

Structures along the Ma & Pa represent a rustic, bygone era. Most of the depots are wooden frame buildings, some with clapboard siding or shingles and some of board-and-batten construction. Perhaps the most picturesque structure on the railroad is the combination station and general office building on Market Street in York. Stone was also a popular building material in this area of the United States, and in the past a number of Ma & Pa buildings, such as the earlier passenger depot in Baltimore, were made of stone. The roundhouse at Baltimore was a combination of stone and wood.

Modeling notes

The tabletop layout presented in this chapter depicts the Maryland & Pennsylvania of today and centers on Ma & Pa's switching operations around York and Red Lion.

By looping the track and creating an upper-tier track level, we can provide for some "mainline" running and include Yoe, Pa., and Dallastown (the latter at the end of a short branch as in the prototype) in the scheme of operation.

Continuous running is possible, but operation will be more prototypical if you run trains point-to-point style; that is, from York to Red Lion and return. Also, a waybill system will make freight-car movement on the Ma & Pa meaningful and more true-to-prototype.

A day's activity on the model Ma & Pa starts as a locomotive eases out of the enginehouse. First stop on the agenda is the PRR (or PC or CR, depending on the era modeled) interchange to pick up cars "left" by the connecting road. Interchange cars destined for York industries are delivered first (while "empty" cars are retrieved) and those destined beyond York are for the time being put in York yard. Empty cars can go to the

Looking in the opposite direction from the grade crossing in the foreground of the photo at the top of the page we see the well-weathered Yoe freighthouse and a rambling office building that probably began life in the late 1800's as a hotel.

M&P and Conrail crews ponder a minor derailment (ex-Penn Central switcher 8512 at far left) at Poorhouse Yard in York on April 1, 1976, the first day of Conrail. M&P 81, 82, and 83 are all present to help with new interchange operations.

One look at this 1940 scene near Woodbine will explain Ma & Pa's need for short-framed locomotives with small drivers. Towing northbound tonnage, Consolidation 41 negotiates one of many tight curves along winding Muddy Creek. Note guardrail.

interchange or to Yoe, to Dallastown, or to Red Lion if they are needed there. Next, the locomotive makes up the train for the southbound run to Red Lion. Because of the facing-point switch position at Dallastown Junction, cars destined for Yoe or Dallastown will have to be pushed ahead of the locomotive or else delivered on the northbound run from Red Lion. When the train returns to York, cars can be forwarded to the PRR interchange and to York industries before the locomotive is retired for the night.

If you have the space (and the time), you may wish to model the entire Ma & Pa as it was in the steam era. If you had the whole York-Baltimore line in your basement, then you might have an operating pattern like this: A passenger train in each direction — this could be either a 4-4-0 or a 4-6-0, baggage-mail cars, and coach, or the gas-electric and a baggage-mail combine — would make the entire run between Baltimore and York. The northbound *York Mail* would carry a couple of milk cars on the head end to be dropped off at milk shipping points; the southbound *Baltimore Mail* would pick up loaded milk cars for delivery to processing plants in Baltimore.

There would be a through freight in each direction, hauled by a heavy 2-8-0, with cars destined to and from the B&O connection at Baltimore and the PRR at York. Two peddler freights hauled by light 2-8-0's would also work the line, one serving the Baltimore-Delta section and the other the York-Delta segment. If the York peddler picked up any cars destined for the B&O interchange at Baltimore, it would leave these at Delta for pickup by the Baltimore peddler. In like fashion, any PRR interchange cars picked up on the south end would be left at Delta for the York peddler.

So there you have it — one of the most classic short lines you can model. Be it steam era or diesel era, the Maryland & Pennsylvania and its quaint heritage offer some of the best modeling possibilities for a layout.

Highway flashers of somewhat unusual construction guard crossings in Red Lion.

Motor car 61 and a baggage-mail trailer are about to depart York in the early 1950's as train No. 2, the middle-of-the-day run to Baltimore.

Upper story of York station houses M&P offices. Automobiles more than anything date some M&P photos because M&P rolling stock and structures remained unchanged for decades. This scene was in 1940.

Bound for Chicago's Loop, CA&E 403 receives passengers on Broadway in Aurora, Ill., in April 1938. The 403 was one of 20 cars (400-419) that Pullman built for the "Roarin' Elgin" in 1923. Aurora street operation ended circa 1940.

Chicago Aurora & Elgin

Traction with variety: "Roarin' Elgin" trains operated along third rail, under wire, over private right of way, in streets, and on Chicago's "L"

SUPER INTERURBANS they were called: the Chicago North Shore & Milwaukee; the Chicago South Shore & South Bend; and the Chicago Aurora & Elgin. Over these three electric lines, once controlled by traction magnate Samuel Insull, a traveler could make his way north, east, or west on frequent, high-speed trains to Milwaukee, the Fox River Valley, or South Bend. Now only the South Shore Line remains. The CA&E died first, ending passenger service in 1957, and the North Shore succumbed in 1963.

Ah yes, the "Roarin' Elgin." At one time, you could board cars at the Loop in downtown Chicago and speed to any of four major cities on the Fox River — Elgin, Geneva, Batavia, and Aurora — with only a minor delay at Wheaton while cars on the train were separated according to their destinations. With service offered to so many western points, it's no wonder the CA&E was also known as the "Sunset Lines."

The Roarin' Elgin began as the Aurora Elgin & Chicago Railway. In 1900 grading was started at Aurora and pushed eastward through Wheaton to Laramie Avenue in Chicago west of the

Car 431 pauses at National Street in Elgin in the early 1950's. Cars 420-434 were built by Cincinnati Car Co. in 1927.

Wood cars survived to the end. Here, two "woods" stop at Villa Avenue in Villa Park. Ovaltine plant is in the background.

A fantrip train on the Batavia branch rolls beneath Illinois Route 25 and Burlington's West Chicago branch in 1939.

68

In Aurora, CA&E trains used a riverfront station that was accessible from a storefront depot (on Broadway), New York Street bridge, and the parking lot.

Aurora streets circa 1911 were alive with detail: ornate store fronts, signs, awnings (one reads ELECTRIC STATION), and trains. The three-car AE&C train will be heading for Chicago shortly, and an EA&S car is heading for Elgin.

business district. In 1902 the line was opened to the public between Chicago (Laramie Avenue), Aurora, and Batavia. The line to Elgin was completed in 1903. Extensive use of third-rail power distribution (something of a novelty in those days) on the new line led to its nickname "The Great Third Rail Route." In 1905, the AE&C obtained trackage rights over the Garfield Park line of the Metropolitan West Side Elevated Railway to a new terminal at Wells Street in Chicago's Loop. In exchange, "L" trains were allowed to use AE&C tracks west from Laramie Avenue to Forest Park, and the AE&C agreed not to carry passengers locally between the Loop and Forest Park.

In 1906 the Elgin, Aurora & Southern Traction Co. lines in and about the Fox River Valley became affiliated with the AE&C. The Fox River Division connected several cities and towns along the Fox River: Aurora, Batavia, Geneva, St. Charles, and Elgin. In 1907 subsidiary Chicago Wheaton & Western was formed to construct a line from Geneva Junction, just west of Wheaton on the Elgin line, to Geneva via West Chicago. At Geneva a direct track connection was made with Fox River lines so cars could operate through from Chicago to St. Charles.

In 1919 the AE&C went into receivership and in 1922 was reorganized as the Chicago Aurora & Elgin Railroad under control of Dr. Thomas Conway Jr. Conway began a rehabilitation project that included stone ballasting, the construction of new automatic substations and a new signal system, and the purchase of steel cars. The Fox River Division became the Aurora, Elgin & Fox River Electric Co. about a year later. In 1926 Samuel Insull purchased the CA&E, but the line again went into receivership during the depression, despite 1-million-dollar-plus improvements by Conway and Insull. Reorganization in 1946 brought a final name change: Chicago Aurora & Elgin Rail*way*.

Overall, CA&E operations remained status quo from the mid-1930's to the 1950's, except for the abandonment of the Geneva line in 1937. Traffic patterns changed after World War II, however, as the five-day work week became more accepted and travel became more rush-hour oriented. But during the 1950's the CA&E met its death, indirectly caused by the Congress Street (now Dwight D. Eisenhower) Expressway being built west out of downtown Chicago. Ironically, it wasn't entirely patronage lost to the new expressway that brought about CA&E's demise, but that expressway construction forced the electric line to lose its downtown terminal. Part of the new expressway was to be built on the right of way of the Garfield Park "L," and planning authorities proposed that CA&E and CTA (Chicago Transit Authority) trains be rerouted downtown via Van Buren Street surface trackage during the expressway's construction (projected to take 5-10 years). CA&E opposed the move because it didn't have the extra equipment to protect lengthened running times — the railroad claimed the rerouting would add almost 30 minutes to train schedules because of numerous street crossings (many of them unguarded, requiring trains to stop and wait for street traffic) and close headways with CTA trains.

A compromise was reached, and in 1953 CA&E trains began using a rebuilt terminal at Forest Park, where an across-the-platform connection was

Two Jewett-built cars on a special movement roll along on what appears to be the Batavia branch.

AE&C built double-end snowplow No. 3 in 1909. At left is a former express car, rebuilt in 1941 to a tool car.

Car 312 at Laramie Avenue shows an intermediate CA&E scheme: body, blue; window band, gray; end doors and windows, red.

Both photos, Edward Frank Jr.

(Above) Express car 9 on the "orchard tracks" at Wheaton yard circa 1937 has two ex-Washington, Baltimore & Annapolis cars in tow. Eight WB&A cars were rebuilt into control trailers. One is shown (below) in front of the Aurora Fire Department.

Collection of George Krambles.

The motorman and passers-by seem to enjoy watching the photographer capture this moment of CA&E history in West Chicago in the middle 1920's. Westbound car 412 is stopped at the station (Public Service building at far right with an electric CA&E sign). A street scene would highlight any CA&E layout.

made with Garfield Park "L" trains using the temporary ground-level route. The transfer at Forest Park and longer commuting times meant the loss of almost half of CA&E's riders within a few months. Hope for reinstatement of single-seat service all the way downtown diminished, and in 1957 the road stopped all passenger service.

Eventually CTA trains began operating to the Loop over tracks in the median strip of the new superhighway, but the CA&E never again entered downtown Chicago. The Roarin' Elgin ended freight service in 1959, and officially abandoned all operations in 1961.

CA&E operations

During the 1920's service generally was provided to Aurora and Elgin every hour, with separate trains departing Chicago every 30 minutes. Cars bound for St. Charles left Chicago approximately every 90 minutes attached to either an Aurora- or Elgin-bound train and separated at Wheaton. Sunday was a peak day of travel in the 1920's as people flocked to the rails for joy rides or excursions to beaches and amusement parks.

During the 1930's half-hour service to Wheaton was typical, with alternate trains continuing beyond to Aurora and Elgin after splitting at Wheaton station. Through cars were operated to Geneva and St. Charles, but passengers bound for Batavia had to transfer to a shuttle car that met mainline trains at Batavia Junction. The Batavia shuttle lasted until the CA&E ceased passenger operations in 1957.

During rush hours, of course, service was more frequent. The little Wells Street terminal must have been a sight to behold at 5 p.m. on a weekday, especially prior to 1952, when rapid-transit trains also used the station. There was very little space for car storage at Wells Street, so most CA&E trains had to be deadheaded several miles west to the Laramie Avenue yards immediately after arrival in Chicago in the morning and deadheaded back just before departure in the evening. In spite of its size (four tracks) Wells Street terminal was one of the busiest stations in Chicago.

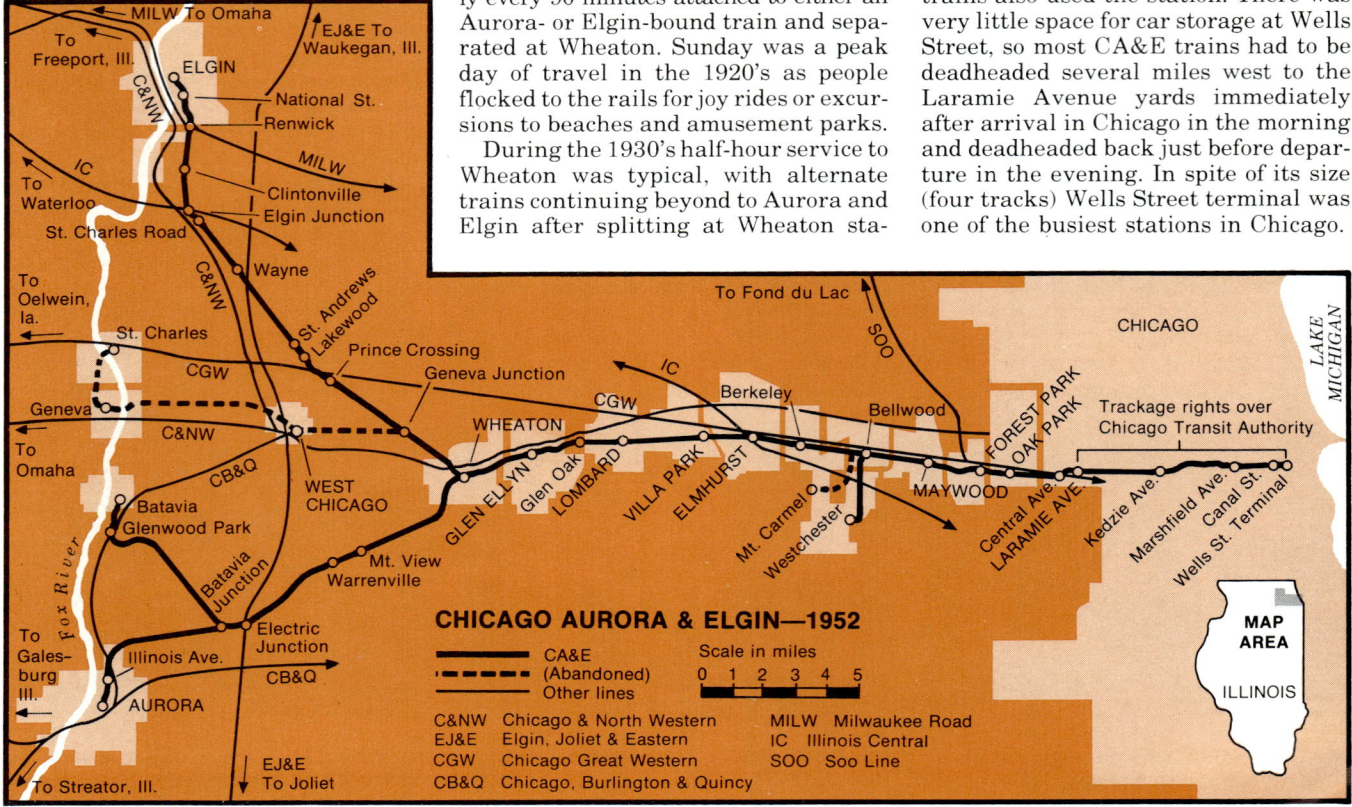

CHICAGO AURORA & ELGIN—1952

▬▬	CA&E
▬ ▬	(Abandoned)
───	Other lines

Scale in miles: 0 1 2 3 4 5

C&NW Chicago & North Western
EJ&E Elgin, Joliet & Eastern
CGW Chicago Great Western
CB&Q Chicago, Burlington & Quincy
MILW Milwaukee Road
IC Illinois Central
SOO Soo Line

MAP AREA ILLINOIS

70

Wheaton yard was one of several primary locations — Aurora, Elgin, and Batavia were some of the others — where trolley wire was used. The original portion of the shop building was constructed in 1902, and an addition was built about 1922.

Henry J. McCord.

General Electric built center-cabs 2001 and 2002 in 1920. CA&E added M.U. connections in 1929 so the two could work in tandem, as they are doing in this April 1957 scene at the Eggert Coal Co. in Elgin. Elgin Watch factory is in the background.

Jim Barrick, collection of Steven P. Hyett.

After World War II, labor costs soared, and eventually most train operations were confined to rush hours. Non-rush hour service to Wheaton was about every 30 minutes, and to Aurora and Elgin every hour. By the mid-1950's, service to Wheaton was about every 45 minutes, and to Aurora and Elgin every 90 minutes. Again, alternate trains ran as a unit to Wheaton where they were split for Elgin and Aurora.

L.c.l. (less-than-carload) freight service began in 1905 on the AE&C using box express motors, but this service proved unsuccessful and simply evolved into "emergency package express service" in the 1920's. The service lasted until CA&E ended operations into the Loop in 1953. However, carrying Chicago newspapers to the suburbs was a lucrative business for the CA&E from 1903 until well after operations had been cut back to Forest Park in 1953. (After 1953, newspapers had to be trucked as far as Forest Park.)

Steam-road interchange began on the CA&E in 1923, but freight service never developed to any great extent because of competition from the steam roads in the area. Most of the CA&E's freight traffic originated at the Ovaltine plant (Wander Company) in Villa Park.

Equipment

Wooden cars from an array of builders — Brill, Jewett, Kuhlman, Stephenson, Niles, Hicks Locomotive Works, and others — were delivered to the AE&C between 1902 and 1914. Many of these wooden beauties lasted until the 1950's, several having been rebuilt. Twelve wooden cars were leased from the North Shore Line in 1936 and purchased in 1946 to handle growing ridership. Two Niles-built parlor-buffet cars, the *Florence* and the *Carolyn*, were delivered to the AE&C in 1905 and 1906. Parlor-dining service did not develop quite as well on the CA&E as it did on the North Shore and South Shore and was given up in 1929. The two parlor-buffets were rebuilt into steel coaches.

Steel cars made their appearance in 1923 during the Conway rehabilitation era when 20 new cars, in a rich red paint scheme with gold leaf striping and lettering, were delivered from Pullman. Nos. 400-419 established a standard design for steel equipment on the CA&E. A second group of cars, Nos. 420-434, delivered by Cincinnati Car Co. in 1927, was nearly identical to the first group. Also in 1927 CA&E purchased one lightweight car from St. Louis Car Company, the 500. More of a streetcar than an interurban, the 500 was intended for the lightly patronized Batavia shuttle, but was sold to the North Shore in 1941. In 1937 and 1938, eight cars were purchased from the defunct Washington, Baltimore & Annapolis. They were rebuilt and used in mainline service as control trailers. In 1945 CA&E received its last new equipment, 10 modern cars from St. Louis Car, Nos. 451-460. These handsome, clean-lined cars were of "fishbelly" design, permitting more spacious seating inside while enabling the car to fit the tight clearances of Chicago's "L" system. Mainstay of the Aurora, Elgin & Fox River Electric were seven cars delivered in 1923 by St. Louis Car, Nos. 300-306; they lasted

The GE twins at Lombard depot, which at one time was also a substation. Note the Miller Beer ad painted on the restaurant's clapboard siding. Don't forget to model the numerous power lines.

Prince Crossing depot/substation (Elgin line) sat north of the tracks at Ingalton Road. The CGW passed over the CA&E beyond the curve. The station still stood in the late 1970's.

Two photos, Edward Frank Jr.

71

Aurora substation marked the changeover point from third rail to overhead wire for the route into Aurora. Some overlap between the two forms of power distribution was necessary at changeover locations.

Edges of high-level passenger platforms in freight territory were hinged to clear freight cars. Edge of right platform, Maywood station, is in normal position; edge of left platform has been flipped up.

A veranda enhanced the handsome Wheaton station, built in 1922 during a modernization program that followed reorganization of the AE&C into the CA&E. Program also included an addition for Wheaton shops.

until the AE&FRE closed in 1935. The cars were sold to the Cleveland Interurban System (later Shaker Heights Rapid Transit).

Between 1902 and 1921 the AE&C/CA&E acquired several express motors from a variety of builders. These were used principally for l.c.l. business. In 1921 and 1922 the line received two General Electric 44-ton steeple-cab locomotives, Nos. 2001 and 2002, followed in 1926 by two Baldwin-Westinghouse center-cabs, Nos. 3003 and 3004. In 1955, rather late in the game, CA&E purchased two 72-ton center-cabs that had been built in 1929 by the Oklahoma Railway. All of these locomotives were used for freight service until 1959. One of the express cars lasted until 1959; the remainder had been built into work equipment or retired. CA&E also owned a number of freight cars and some work equipment.

Physical plant

The CA&E outlived most other U. S. interurban systems because it was more a suburban operation than a city-to-city interurban. The line had a high-speed entrance into Chicago, served the booming West Side, and for the most part utilized private right of way.

Third-rail distribution of 600-volt d.c. was used almost exclusively except where tracks invaded urban areas in Aurora, Elgin, Batavia, Geneva, and West Chicago. Both trolley wire and third rail were used in Wheaton yard. In earlier years CA&E produced its own

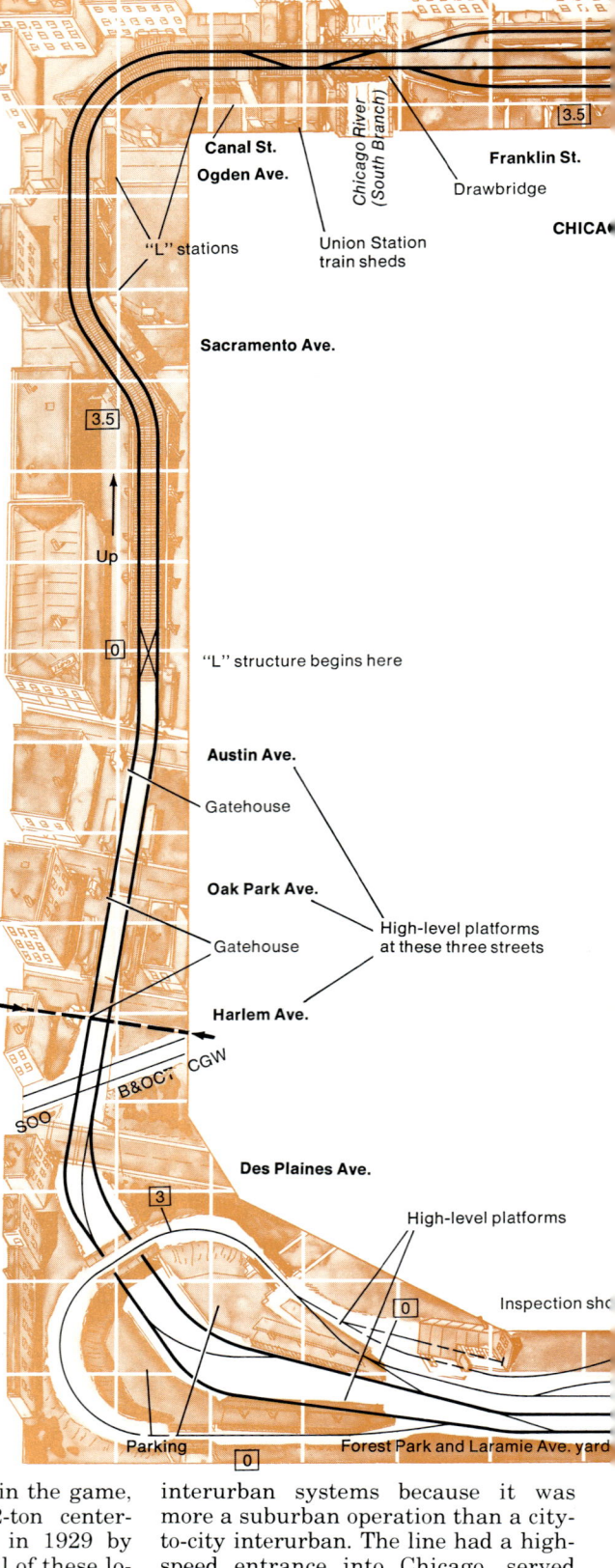

72

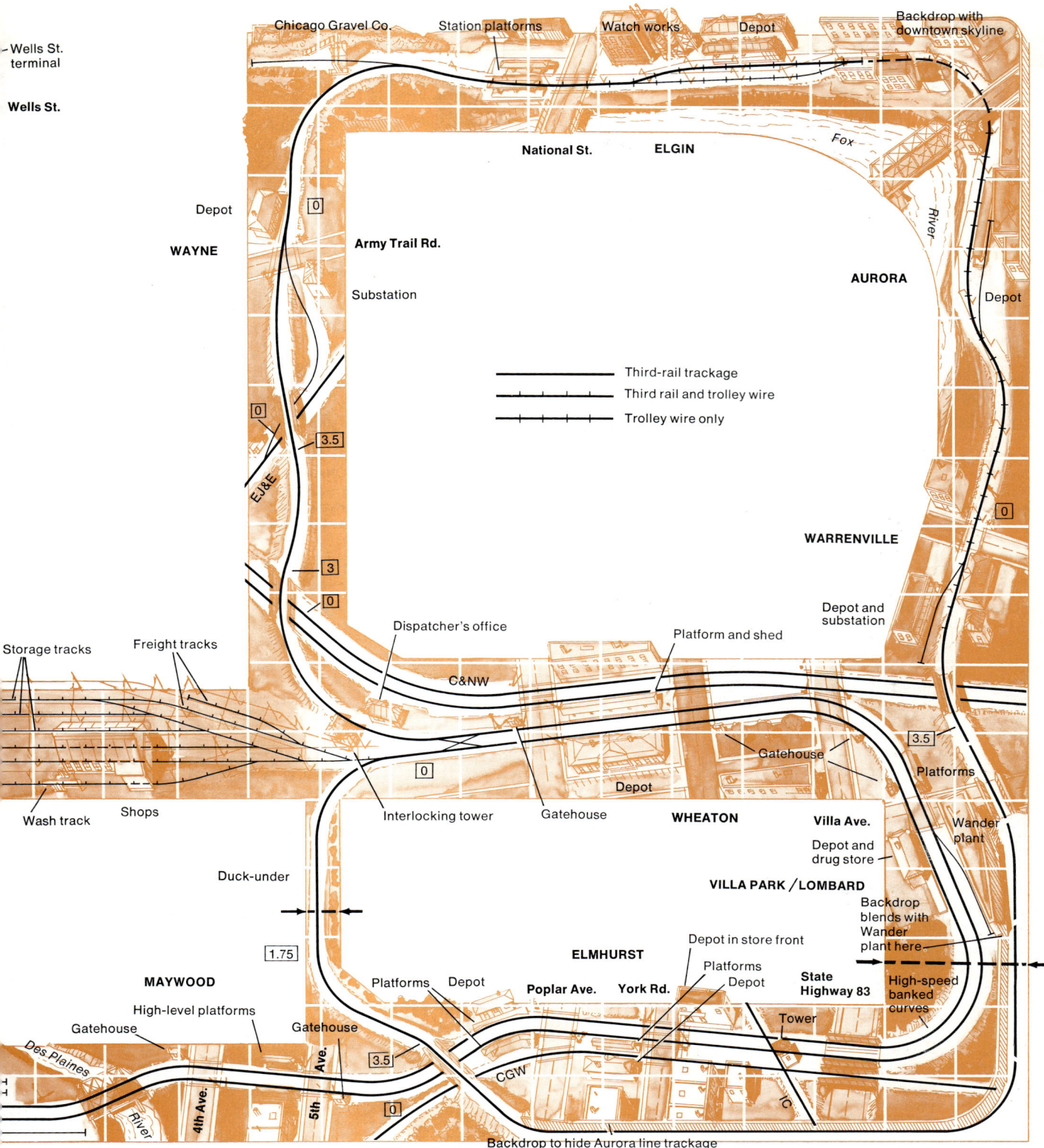

power in a coal-fired, steam-powered generating station at Batavia, from which power was distributed to substations throughout the system. Later the railroad bought power from the Public Service Company of Northern Illinois (Commonwealth Edison). High-speed train movements over the heavy, well-ballasted CA&E tracks were protected by automatic color-light block signals.

As with the North Shore and the South Shore, grades were no problem in this lake-basin prairie region of the Midwest. The only significant climbs were out of the Fox River Valley — no problem for electric traction. Most intersecting rail lines were crossed in typical interurban fashion — by means of grade separation, although there were a few grade-level crossings.

Heading west from Wells terminal, CA&E trains traversed the Garfield Park "L" to Laramie Avenue where the tracks dropped to street level. At Laramie Avenue there was a storage yard and inspection shop.

Between Laramie and Des Plaines avenues was an interesting stretch of track that should warrant modeling on any CA&E layout. This busy segment of double-track main crossed numerous streets at grade, all spaced about a block apart and all protected by manually operated crossing gates.

Just east of Des Plaines Avenue in Forest Park, where the CTA had turning facilities, the main line made a reverse curve and crossed at grade the busy double-track line used by Balti-

73

A Chicago-bound CA&E train has just departed the Sacramento Avenue "L" station. Elevated right of way certainly would take longer to model than ground-level trackage, but the results would be rewarding. "L" structure could be built with plastic bridge and structural components and stripwood.

CA&E trains intermingled with rapid-transit cars between Forest Park and downtown Chicago. CA&E used rapid-transit tracks from Laramie Avenue east to Wells Street at the Loop; in exchange, rapid-transit trains used CA&E tracks west from Laramie to Forest Park. This is Marshfield Junction near the Loop.

more & Ohio Chicago Terminal, Soo Line, and Chicago Great Western. Street crossings west of Des Plaines through the communities of Maywood, Bellwood, Elmhurst, Villa Park, Glen Ellyn, and Wheaton were less numerous. Many of them were protected by automatic gates, flashers, and even a couple of old-fashioned wigwag signals. In some of the suburbs, the CA&E main line (as well as the paralleling Chicago & North Western main in some places) enjoyed a prominent location in passing through the city — right through the center of the business district in a fenced-off right of way.

CA&E had some handsome depots, and famous Wheaton station (that's where most CA&E enthusiasts seemed to congregate to take photographs) was a classic example. Built in 1922, this handsome brick structure served as a combined depot and transportation office, and featured window awnings, verandas, and landscaping. Passengers alighting from outbound trains were protected by platform sheds.

High-level platforms were found at many CA&E stations, notably those at Elgin, Batavia, Batavia Junction, Aurora, and all stations east of Bellwood. Most high-level platforms had hinged edges to allow for the passage of freight equipment. As freight trains eased past these platforms, a brakeman on the front of the engine would flip up the edge sections with a pole, and a crewman on the rear of the train would flip them back down as the train cleared. All this was accomplished without stopping the train!

Batavia Junction, used mainly as a transfer point, was but a shelter and a set of platforms. In later years, terminals in Elgin, Aurora, and Batavia were reached via riverfront trackage, thus avoiding street operation. Depots at these cities were merely storefront properties, and passengers boarded trains from high-level platforms which were reached by going out the back door of the station.

Modeling notes

The advantage of modeling a traction line is that you can squeeze more model railroading into a given amount of space. We felt the CA&E could best be adapted to a shelf-type layout (which utilizes space very efficiently) with a dioramalike presentation of scenery and structures.

This versatile layout can be operated as a point-to-point system, a point-to-loop layout, or a loop-to-loop circuit. The layout emphasizes CA&E's double-

Scale modeled		Z	N	TT	HO	S	O
Spacing of rulings	in.	4.50	6.00	9.00	12.00	18.00	24.00
Space horizontally	ft.-in.	9-6	12-0	17-0	22-0	33-0	44-0
Space vertically	ft.-in.	8-6	10-0	13-0	16-0	24-0	32-0
Minimum radius	in.	4.50	6.00	9.00	12.00	18.00	24.00
Parallel straight track spacing	in.	.63	.87	1.16	1.60	2.18	2.90
Parallel curved track spacing	in.	1.09	1.50	1.99	2.75	3.74	4.98
Multiply elevations by	in.	.40	.54	.73	1.00	1.36	1.81

Turnouts: unless otherwise indicated, No. 4 in all scales

Spacing of rulings	mm.	112.50	150.00	225.00	300.00	450.00	600.00
Space horizontally	m.	2.85	3.60	5.10	6.60	9.90	13.20
Space vertically	m.	2.55	3.00	3.90	4.80	7.20	9.60
Minimum radius	mm.	113.00	150.00	225.00	300.00	450.00	600.00
Parallel straight track spacing	mm.	16.00	22.00	29.00	40.00	54.00	73.00
Parallel curved track spacing	mm.	27.00	37.00	50.00	69.00	93.00	125.00
Multiply elevations by	mm.	10.00	14.00	18.00	25.00	34.00	45.00

Horizontal and vertical dimensions of this layout allow for a minimum aisleway width of 24". To maintain this minimum aisleway width when using TT or smaller scales, the layout should be expanded at the suggested locations indicated by dashed lines.

So that all areas of a model railroad remain accessible, no portion of a layout should be more than 30" (75 cm.) from an aisleway or access opening. Thus, when constructing a layout to Railroad You Can Model track-plan dimensions in a scale larger than HO, it may be necessary to add access openings or lift-out scenery sections where not already shown.

The Batavia shuttle waits at Batavia Junction for a train from Chicago in 1943.

74

St. Louis Car built CA&E's final equipment order — and one of the last car orders for the interurban industry as a whole: 10 cars delivered in 1945. Above, two of the smart-lined, scarlet-and-gray cars arrive off the Elgin line past Wheaton tower in 1949.

track Chicago-Wheaton route, with its "L" structures, ground-level trackage, and numerous street crossings.

As with any layout that depicts a prototype operation, it is necessary to use modeler's license to select, condense, and change prototype aspects to fit our limitations. For example, we have combined Forest Park with Laramie Avenue yards. If you model the post-1953 CA&E, when travelers transferred to CTA trains at Forest Park, you'll want to include the optional loop for CA&E trains to use to return to Wheaton. The loop at Forest Park permits continuous operation, because the line to Aurora and Elgin is actually one big loop.

If you want to duplicate pre-1953 prototype point-to-point operations, this can be done, too. A typical four-car train would start at Wells Street terminal in Chicago and separate into two 2-car trains at Wheaton, one train continuing to Elgin and the other to Aurora. If you have the space you may wish to add the Batavia shuttle for extra interest and operation. There are enough sidings and interchanges on the layout for a modest freight operation, but there is room to add more industry if you have a special interest in traction freight.

For an interesting operating session with fellow modelers, give one person responsibility for the Chicago-Forest Park segment with its intermingling CTA and CA&E movements; another person can control Forest Park-Wheaton operations, including the yard. A third man could handle Wheaton-Aurora/Elgin trains, and a fourth person could be kept very busy operating all the crossing gates on the layout!

For more detailed information about traction modeling, refer to Kalmbach's TRACTION GUIDEBOOK FOR MODEL RAILROADERS.

Elmhurst rated three stations: Poplar Avenue, York Street, and Spring Road. The Chicago local is pulling away from the York Street shelter. The station at left in the background belonged to the CGW, which paralleled the CA&E through town. By 1978, the CA&E right of way had become the Illinois Prairie Path bikeway, and the CGW tracks, too, had been torn up.

75

Bibliography

TRACK PLANNING FOR RAILROADS YOU'D LIKE TO MODEL — Based on "A track plan for the Genesee & Wyoming" by Linn H. Westcott, MODEL RAILROADER, December 1976. Text revision by Mike Schafer.

MONON — Based on "X marks the spot" by Andy Anderson, MODEL TRAINS, August 1954. Text revision and new track plan by Gary Dolzall and Mike Schafer. Bibliography: Barriger, John W., Hungerford, Edward, Kalmbach, A. C., and Westcott, Linn H., special Monon issue of TRAINS, July 1947; Dubin, Arthur D., MORE CLASSIC TRAINS. Kalmbach, Milwaukee, 1974; "Locomotives of Chicago, Indianapolis & Louisville Ry." *Railroad Stories*, January 1933; *Monon News & Notes*, Huntington, Ind. Acknowledgments: Montford L. Switzer; Dennis Wozniczka.

GRAHAM COUNTY RAILROAD — Based on "Shay-operated short line: a railroad you can model" by Michael J. Dunn III, MODEL RAILROADER, April 1962. Text revision by Mike Schafer; new track plan by Richard Francaviglia. Bibliography: Ferrell, Mallory Hope, "Sidewiders and a singing engineer." TRAINS, January 1962; Reid, H., "Passengers for the Graham County." TRAINS, August 1966. Acknowledgements: Thomas R. Ebright and R. D. Ranger, Graham County Railroad; Morgan C. McIlwain; Louis Saillard.

B & M'S GLOUCESTER BRANCH — Text and track plan by George H. Drury. Acknowledgments: Kenneth E. Patton; Jack Towne.

McCLOUD RIVER RAILROAD — Based on "The McCloud River RR" by Donald Sims, MODEL TRAINS, Summer 1959. Text revision and new track plan by George H. Drury. Bibliography: Benson, Ted, "Steam below Shasta." TRAINS, October 1971; Hanft, Robert M., *Pine Across the Mountain*. Golden West, San Marino, Calif., 1970; Sims, Donald, "Logging line, 1959 model." TRAINS, February 1959. Acknowledgments: Ted Benson; Don Hansen.

PRR'S HORSESHOE CURVE — Based on "Pennsy's famous Horseshoe Curve" by Andy Anderson, MODEL TRAINS, November 1954. Text revision and new track plan by Mike Schafer. Bibliography: Burgess, George H., and Kennedy, Miles C., *Centennial History of the Pennsylvania Railroad Company*. Pennsylvania Railroad, Philadelphia, 1949; Morgan, David P., "World's busiest mountain railroad." TRAINS, April 1957; Sohlberg, Harry T., "Horseshoe Curve." TRAINS, March 1941; "Horseshoe Curve and approach to Gallitzin Tunnels." TRAINS & TRAVEL, May 1952.

MILWAUKEE ROAD'S BEER LINE — Based on "The Beer Line" by Andy Anderson, MODEL TRAINS, April 1955. Text revision and new track plans by George H. Drury. Bibliography: Abbey, Wallace W., "The Beer Line that made Milwaukee famous." TRAINS & TRAVEL, August 1952; Martin, Boyce, "Cement Plant Railroad." MODEL RAILROADER, June 1952. Acknowledgments: Brian Holtz, Joseph Schlitz Brewing Company.

WHITE PASS & YUKON — Based on "Modeling the White Pass & Yukon" by John Armstrong, MODEL RAILROADER, March 1953. Text revision and Rio Grande track plan by George H. Drury; WP&Y plan by John Armstrong. Bibliography: Jaques, F. L., "Gateway to the Yukon." TRAINS, January 1951; Morgan, David P., "TRAINS goes to Alaska." TRAINS, February and March 1963.

MARYLAND & PENNSYLVANIA — Based on "The heritage of the Ma & Pa" by Bill Rau, MODEL RAILROADER, May 1965. Text revision and new track plan by Mike Schafer. Bibliography: Hilton, G. W., *The Ma & Pa – A history of the Maryland & Pennsylvania Railroad*. Howell-North, Berkeley, Calif., 1963; Moedinger, William Jr., "The Ma & Pa." TRAINS, December 1941. Acknowledgments: Glenn E. Dietz.

CHICAGO AURORA & ELGIN — Based on "The Roarin' Elgin" by Andy Anderson, MODEL TRAINS, February 1955. Text revision and new track plan by Mike Schafer. Bibliography: Central Electric Railfans' Association, *The Great Third Rail* (Bulletin 105). Chicago, 1961; Gregory, William, and St. Clair, Robert, "The Roarin' Elgin heads for trouble." TRAINS & TRAVEL, January 1952; Hilton, G. W., and Due, John F., *The Electric Interurban Railways in America*. Stanford University, Stanford, Calif., 1960; Middleton, William D., THE INTERURBAN ERA. Kalmbach, Milwaukee, 1961. Acknowledgments: Edward Frank Jr.; Steven P. Hyett; George Krambles, Chicago Transity Authority; Fred H. Lonnes, R.E.L.I.C. trolley museum.

Additional information obtained from numerous issues of *Extra 2200 South*, Cincinnati; *Moody's Transportation Manual*, Moody's Investors Service, New York; *Official Guide of the Railways*, National Railway Publication Company, New York; and *Poor's Manual of Railroads*, Poor's Publishing Company, New York.